This book belongs to

ASK THE
College
Counselor

**Every Family's Guide to College Admissions
and Putting Your Best Story Forward**

Brady Norvall

Ask the College Counselor by Brady Norvall
Cover and internal design by Laura Sucre

Typefaces used:
Modern Era, Freight Text

Library of Congress Number: 2026900569

eBook 978-1-959009-34-4
Paperback 978-1-959009-35-1

Published in the United States by Simply Good Press, Montclair, N.J.

To Lily and Luna, our daughters, who make me laugh forever, and grateful even longer. You are the muchy much that my soul always needs. I am always so proud to be your dad.

To all the university admission officers and high school counselors who bust their butts every day to make this process better for young people by being kind and compassionate (and who push for transparency).

Foreword

When I reflect on our family's journey through the college admissions process, I'm immediately grateful to the friend who introduced me to Brady. From our very first conversation over a decade ago, I was struck by his combination of insight, empathy, and experience. His philosophy resonated deeply with me: that every student has a voice worth hearing, and that college admissions can be a time of growth and reflection—not just a race for prestige. He didn't see college as a prize to be won, but as part of a young person's larger journey of becoming.

Brady wasn't just a college advisor to our family. He became a true partner and friend. He walked alongside both of our kids—and us as parents—as they navigated their post-high school decisions. He brought calm when things felt overwhelming, and humor when we needed a reminder to breathe. Most importantly, he saw our children clearly, believed in them deeply, and helped them believe in themselves. Throughout it all, he reminded us that this process isn't just about getting into a school—it's about helping young people become the thoughtful, grounded adults they're meant to be.

That's what makes this book so special. It's not just a practical step by step guide (though it absolutely is). It carries Brady's voice and reflects the way he approaches this work: with care, with perspective, and with deep respect for students and their families. Whether you're trying to make sense of rankings, figure out the difference between a college and a university, trying to understand the role of a school counselor, or simply want to know how to support your child through it all, you'll find something meaningful here.

As a parent, I want my children to be independent, self-aware, and resilient. I also know we don't get there on our own. Mentors matter—at every age. Brady's guidance has shaped not only our children's educational paths, but how we think as a family about growth, decision-making, and the future.

This book holds the same clarity, warmth, and wisdom that Brady has shared with us over the years. I hope it brings you the same sense of steadiness, insight, and encouragement.

We're so grateful for him—and I'm glad this book found its way to you.

Warmly,
Deborah Lake
CO-FOUNDER, 4EARTH FARMS

"*Ask the College Counselor* embodies respect for all parties, understands holistic needs, has an acute awareness of the ever-changing application landscape, is always in listening mode, and, above all, places the emotional and logistical needs of each student at the heart of planning. Through this published offering, Mr. Norvall assuredly exposes parents and carers (and even school officials!) to more poignant definitions and explanations of the various substrata underpinning the college application process and how to navigate potential murky waters. His contribution to this ongoing dialogue comes at a very sensitive but necessary juncture in the history of college advice and guidance and is a most welcome addition. Many of your doubts will be clarified, preconceptions cleared, and questions answered. Enjoy the discovery process as a family if you can."

– Dr. Barry Hallinan, Senior Master, St. Paul's School, Sao Paulo, Brazil

"Working with Brady during the college processes of my three children was the best decision we could have made for them. Not only is he incredibly knowledgeable but, most importantly, he built a strong relationship based on empathy and confidence. Brady is the kind of person that listens to young adults and has the ability to understand everything that is left unsaid. He sees what is behind their words and acknowledges their feelings."

– Leandra and Renato Auriemo

"Sadly, it is quite common for the interplay between high school college counselors and Independent Educational Consultants to be a difficult one. In that respect, Brady Norvall is a breath of fresh air. He exemplifies the ideal qualities that make such partnerships successful. Brady understands the importance of placing students at the center of the process and respects the role and expertise of school-based college counselors. Working with Brady is easy because he values the importance of coordination and always prioritizes the best interests of the students, which ultimately enhances the college application experience for everyone involved."

– Augusto Neto, Director of Careers and University Guidance, The American School of Rio de Janeiro, Brazil; Times Higher Education International Schools Advisory Board Member; Times Higher Education Global Awardee for Global Counsellor of the Year, 2025.

"Brady helps students navigate which schools fit best for their needs, location, size, and interest. His perspective of guiding students to choose what is best for them gives parents peace of mind. Everyone has an opinion about this process, but Brady's experience and kindness are invaluable."

– Vinny and Victoria Smith

"Brady's knowledge of people and this process is fundamental. Understanding schools and programs was not easy for me, as a foreigner, and Brady was great at helping me realize options and understand how my own interests translate to university environments. He helped me comprehend what program fit my whole self. However, his true expertise comes from getting his students to believe in themselves in a time of stress and anxiety. Brady helped me gain confidence in a time it was much needed."

– Eduardo L, Co-Founder Media4Equity

"We have known Brady for 18+ years and have placed our full trust in his college counseling and mentoring. He is an outstanding professional who has had a profound impact on our family. He has been not only a counselor but also a mentor and dear friend, becoming one of the most positively influential people in our youngest daughter's life. Beyond his professional expertise, Brady and his family have become an extension of our own. We deeply appreciate his wisdom, dedication, and kindness and hiring him was one of the best decisions we ever made. Let this book serve your family as an extension of his knowledgeable, compassionate, and deeply committed counseling for teens and families."

– Malu and Alberto Duhau

"I met Brady at one of the lowest points of my life, at a dead-end school, in a dead-end town, with dead-end friends, and no way out. Point being, I was stuck, depressed, scared, and I wanted him to bail me out. Except he didn't. Not to get too meta, but to put a quote inside a quote "give a man a fish, and you'll feed him for a day. Now, teach a man to fish, and he will get with all the women in the small fishing village." I don't remember which philosopher said that one, but Brady basically showed me that I could dig myself out of my own hole, which I did. I was able to transfer from a zero school to a top-5 screenwriting program. But more importantly, Brady was the first person to really empower me with my writing. No one had ever told me that I was the best writer they had ever worked with. And whether that was a lie or not, hell I believed him. So, I believed in myself."

– Max Civita

"*Ask the College Counselor* reflects the same guidance that helped my daughters find the right colleges where they grew both academically and personally, after I first met Brady in São Paulo as an experienced counselor who soon became a trusted friend and part of our family. With its caring nature, exquisite humor, and insightful advice, this book helps families navigate the complex journey of higher education."

– Silvia Fernandez

Contents

Intro

Part I: The Role of a Private College Advisor

Part II: Quick Facts: Universities and Colleges

The Application Process

Finances

The Teen's Guide to the Admissions Essay

Additional Resources

This book is for anyone with a student who is about to enter high school, or is in high school, and wants to understand as much about the process of applying to universities as I can generally explain. Some people have been encouraging me to write this book for almost 20 years (thanks Jofi!), and others have asked me if I can put my lessons about applying to university into a concise roadmap. Hopefully, in the pages ahead, you will find guidance and answers to questions that you have, and that you didn't yet realize were important to consider.

I am certainly not writing this book to encourage anyone toward any specific course of action. Some families might read this and extrapolate that they do, indeed, want to seek out private help. Others, perhaps, will feel like this book itself allowed them to feel more comfortable about building a positive relationship with the school counselor, and that is enough. Whatever you decide for your family is good. As much as this process is about helping a family understand universities, programs of study, and the application process, the help itself has to be directed toward the young person. Unfortunately or not, parents are oftentimes in their own way when it comes to highly emotional situations, and there are very few things in life which are more charged than adolescence and a young person's transition from high school to … whatever comes after. In this regard, I hope this book helps you feel grounded and a bit more confident about how to move forward in order to find the best information and with the clearest intentions to help your student feel supported.

Again, you may seek the services of a private advisor, or you may choose not to. Either way, people undertaking this process of applying to university will have input coming from somewhere (typically from MANY places and often conflicting), perhaps a teacher, parents of friends, neighbors, grandparents, coaches, not to mention chat groups and message boards. Whether any of this is accurate- or welcome- is another story. In that regard, this book will offer some direction and transparency to help anyone navigate the years ahead by focusing on the things which really matter, such as grades, picking challenging courses, and pursuing creative expression, while not putting much stake in those things that don't matter at all like expensive summer programs, pay-to-play honor societies, overemphasized test prep, and specific major selection.

The truth is that throughout the high school years, far too many people are going to start expressing their opinions, trying to influence- not necessarily with bad intentions, of course- the path that a young person should choose. In this book, there are not a lot of "shoulds". Hopefully, there are some really valuable insights, and perhaps even some answers that might help anyone navigate the choices ahead by allowing you to see those choices more clearly and prioritize what is really most meaningful.

No university is perfect. But every campus I have ever been to, more than 350+ and counting, offers aspects that encourage growth and learning.

I am confident that this book will give each reader something valuable and help them have a smoother, more well-informed process from now to ... whatever comes next.

Brady

Intro

What does a private college advisor do? On the surface, the answer is simple. A private advisor is an expert who guides a student and their family through the transition from high school into university. They help tackle the many practical concerns of the application process, like choosing the right school, knowing when to apply, and figuring out the college essay(s). This simple explanation is accurate, and the practical considerations are, of course, all important.

However, if you look deeper, there's another aspect to the job that is less tangible but may be the most vital role that a college advisor plays, and that is the role of mentor. As much as a private college advisor is here to answer practical questions, they're also able to provide a young person with support and guidance at an intimidating milestone in their life.

You see, when we talk about admission to university, we're really discussing two separate things: first, a rite of passage into adulthood. And second, a continuation of education and a maturing into a deeper understanding of the self. It is imperative not to conflate the two. When we do, we fall into the trap of treating admission itself as the accomplishment, the completion of the student's identity development. We assume that the student will metamorphose into an adult through sheer proximity to the university.

Admission is just another beginning. University is the time for a young person to build on their experiences, to grow their understanding of what they value and why. When young people treat admission as a reward they must live up to, they get to university afraid to explore and make mistakes. But admission to university is like entry into a theme park—you get to choose your adventure. There is no singular path toward success. What success means is personal, something that is developed from one's values and beliefs. This process of transitioning from high school to life beyond, be it college/university or something else, is a time when we can re-evaluate ourselves. For young people experiencing this, the opportunity to have positive role models is invaluable. A personal education advisor can help a student articulate what their values are and help them understand how those values can inform their goals for their education- and their life- beyond university.

Young people need more positive role models in their lives. If any of us think back on our own experiences, chances are we can recall one person (at least) who empowered us, boosted our confidence, acknowledged our efforts, and taught us to take pride in ourselves. These are the people who believe in us, even though they don't have to. But because they do, their faith in us helps us believe in ourselves. Unfortunately, young people have increasingly fewer relationships now that allow them to express vulnerability and build trust through honesty and openness. Alas, discussing that question would be an entirely other book: increasingly-narrow cultural definition of "success"; hyper-competitivity; hyper-connectivity; our society asks too much of teachers and educators while paying them too little; cultish obsession with certain university brands.

> **"Families hire IEC's or private college advisors for a host of motivations. What's consistent across any, though, is the understanding that their child needs as much support and guidance as they can get during the application, and transition, from high school to college/university."**

This is why a private college advisor's job is not only dispensing practical information or looking over a college admissions essay. The process is a conduit, helping the student formulate their conception of their identity as a young adult. It's a chance for them to express themselves through their interests and tell their personal narrative. They get to articulate who their friends are, what relationships they value, the types of people they want to spend time with, and the types of people they prefer not to be around. As the student goes through this process and thinks about their goals in this next step of their education, they're thinking deeply, perhaps for the first time, about what is means to cultivate a life that is meaningful to them. Over time, this idea of importance can shift. That which we value at 17 years old, or 20, is supposed to change. Life requires us to adapt to our own growth and discovery, to assess our previous positions and accept that unlearning information is sometimes required to become a better, more complete human. Thinking deeply about such things will never be harmful.

Of course, successful admission to college/university is the goal, but it must be said that creating a young person who is their own champion and can advocate for themselves is, in fact, an elemental part of the process for the transition to university (and life, in general).

PART ONE

The Role of a Private College Advisor

Before you can decide whether a private college advisor is the right choice for you, it's important to understand what role a private advisor plays and what kind of help they can, and can't, offer.

Q: Why hire a private college advisor?

Families hire IEC's or private college advisors for a host of motivations. What's consistent across any, though, is the understanding that their child needs as much support and guidance as they can get during the application, and transition, from high school to college/university.

For many high school seniors, college admissions is the biggest, most intensive challenge they've had to face. There are a lot of moving parts, from test prep to summer programs, budgetary concerns and financial aid, essay writing, acquiring recommendations, and thinking about majors and programs of study. And all these concerns pale in comparison to the monumental task of just choosing where to apply, from the thousands of universities in the U.S. and abroad. There's a lot of ambiguity and uncertainty baked into the whole process, and it can be deeply overwhelming, not only for the student but the whole family.

Unfortunately, with all the uncertainty, families also experience a lot of conflict during this process. Students experience pressure from all sides, they get conflicting advice, or no advice at all, and they get overloaded with the input of others. They don't know where to begin, so they avoid doing so. Young people are frustrated. Families are frustrated. Communication breaks down. The whole ordeal starts to seem impossible, with student just spinning their wheels on experiences and activities that they may have heard will make them a stronger applicant. It's just so difficult to get really clear, objective guidance for this process that has come to feel highly secretive and uncertain.

So, what does a private college advisor offer?

First, they are someone with a lot of experience surrounding the college application process. They can act as the voice of knowledge to dispel the uncertainty and ambiguity that you and your student may be struggling with. They can answer any questions you or your child have, either about the application process, itself, or about the transition from high school to college, including orientations, move-ins, major and program choices, and general transition advice. If you don't have experience with higher education, or your student doesn't have access to a school counselor, a private advisor can give you more in-depth understanding about universities, in general, and the different institutions and programs available.

Second, a private college advisor can winnow the application process down into smaller steps to help your teenager break through application paralysis. They can help your teen figure out where to start and then, subsequently, lay out a reasonable timeline so that you, as the parent, don't have to be their project manager (which never goes well).

Third, they come in as a third party with no preconceived notions or expectations of your student. As a mentor, an advisor's aim is not to tell a student what they should do, but rather to listen to them and support them as they learn to navigate the system for themselves. They are there to prompt your teen and guide them to a place of greater self-awareness as they consider what their strengths and weaknesses are, what they're interested in, and what would be a good fit for them. Ultimately, the hope is for the student, themselves, to be able to articulate their goals and plan the steps that will get them from the present moment to where they want to be, with as much sound information as possible.

Finally, a private advisor is someone who bridges expectations and opens lines of communication between 1) the parent and the student, 2) the student and the school, and 3) the student and the universities they're considering. They ensure that the parent is informed and feels as connected to the process as they truly wish to be, while also giving the student the space to learn how to navigate challenges independently. In other words, my job, and one of the goals of this book, is to make sure that everyone can enter- and undertake- this journey with sound information and a valuable foundation of knowledge. This book will help to fill-in any information gaps.

There's an analogy I like to use with parents to describe what I do. Some may find the scenario familiar. Imagine you have a teen whose room is wildly messy. You ask them to go clean up, but walk by a little while later only to find them somewhere in their room just staring around, paralyzed by how and where to begin. It's not that they don't know how to put things away. It's not that they don't know where everything goes. It's not that they don't know what's clean or dirty. It's that the mess feels so big that they don't know where to start. At this point, you as the advisor come in and say, "Hey, let's start over here in this corner. Let's put all these clothes away." And then as they complete that, you say, "Now let's do the desk, and then your bed." And as you nudge them along, they start to figure out what to do next, on their own. Teenagers learn how to tackle these small problems individually, by being shown and led. At the same time, this process isn't as simple as a messy room. Students haven't seen it before, let alone dealt with it. So that's part of why the college application process feels so enormous. It is big, don't get me wrong. But in no way is it insurmountable.

Q: How is a private college advisor different from a school counselor?

While you might expect the school counselor and private college advisor to fulfill, more or less, the same role, the two actually have tangibly different parts to play in the college application process. However, it would be fair to say that both have the same ultimate concern, which is to ensure that each student in their care is set up to succeed when transitioning from high school to college.

Both, counselors and private advisors, help students and families understand the necessary parts of a college application, keep them motivated and communicating, and provide clarity around the practical aspects of higher education such as funding, or the differences between institution types (for example, universities and community colleges). How the two roles differ is also important for any family to understand.

School counselors are instrumental. At the same time, they are responsible for many students at once, which naturally limits the amount of time they are able to dedicate to any given student or single family. Of absolute importance, the school counselor provides students with the data they need to use as a jumping-off point, otherwise known as the "School Profile", which is the school's application and acceptance/rejection history. For example, a counselor can show a student the general admissions trends over the previous few years, including what percentage of applicants each university has admitted from that particular high school, and whether any of those admitted applicants have a profile similar to this particular student. They can also detail whether the admitted applicants from previous years applied during an early round or regular decision, and help the student understand where they stand within the overall year group of their high school class. Even for schools that don't rank, a school counselor is able to give an initial assessment as to whether a student's choice of classes is considered rigorous enough for certain universities. If a student is really interested in a specific school, the counselor can tell them the number of students from their high school that were admitted to that university in previous years. From there, the student can further explore their options on their own, with the knowledge of where they have the best chance of admission. All of this information is valuable and the school counselor is the only one who possesses it.

The other large part of a school counselor's responsibilities is to act as a liaison between the student applicant and the university. They generally have contacts (or can make contact) at each university, and can arrange for a student to speak with an admissions officer at any school of particular interest. They're also responsible for writing letters of recommendation for students—but more on that later.

A counselor is also someone students can go to for advice on their admissions essay. For example, if a student needs help with topic ideas or wants some insight regarding their initial brainstorm, a school counselor is a fantastic sounding board. Additionally, when the essay is going through a final review process, the counselor should be happy to be a final pair of eyes. All told, school counselors are helpful to consult at the beginning and end of each step. They make sure that each student has help with the broad strokes of the application process. For many students, this is what is needed. For others, a private advisor complements the school counselor and is able to pick up where the school counselor leaves off.

Now, if a school counselor is responsible for the broad strokes, it's a private advisor that provides support on the finer details.

In contrast to the large workload of any school counselor, private advisors will typically work with a smaller number of students at a time, which means they have more resource not only for each individual student but also for the families of those students. (Note: this isn't to say that your student's school counselor won't meet with you if requested, but these meetings are, by necessity, limited in number.) A private advisor acts as a regular point of contact, someone that a student and their family can turn to for support, advice, and guidance on a day-to-day basis.

Because private advisors are a more accessible presence, they can be a resource for students with granular questions about the college applications. A student might ask a private advisor for help in articulating one specific point in their admissions essay, for example, or get advice on the way to present their extracurricular activities for the most impact.

Meeting on a regular basis also means private advisors get to know their students quite well and have a unique perspective when counseling them through their process of understanding aptitudes and interests, and how this might align with potential majors and, thus, universities. In counterpoint to the more data-focused approach of a school counselor, private advisors can advise on the more subjective, personal considerations a student may have, such as campus culture or the best schools for a student's specific learning style. These difficult-to-quantify details make a real difference to a university experience, but a student researching potential schools may not know what to look for. As an expert that also understands the student's needs and goals, a private counselor is someone who can point them in the right direction. They can also use the extra time they get with their students to help them cast a "wider net" when looking at potential schools.

Where the responsibilities of a school counselor and a private advisor do overlap, the overlap doesn't have to be a power struggle. In fact, the overlap should ideally work to the benefit of the student, who can be certain that they're well-informed on all aspects of the college application process. When a family has questions or concerns, having the school counselor validate the advice of the private advisor or vice versa can be very reassuring.

And of course, at their best, both counselors, school and private, work in concert to empower a student, boost their confidence, and help them achieve greater outcomes.

I had a student recently, let's call him Ben. In conversations, we talked about what Ben was looking for in a college and made a list of schools that made sense for him based on his profile and his interests and lifestyle. There was one school in particular that Ben was really excited about, but no one from his high school had ever applied there. The issue with having no prior applicants is that there is no data, no history, nothing from which we could draw some useful information which compares his academic profile to other, previous applicants and admitted students. Rather than be discouraged, Ben went to his school counselor and explained why he was so interested in that university, laying out all the aspects Ben had researched and become excited about, including much of what we had been discussing for weeks. He then asked his school counselor for support.

This counselor sprang into action, reached out to the appropriate admissions officer at the institution, indicating that there was an outstanding young student who was expressing interest, and acknowledging that the school counselor isn't able to provide a lot of help in this particular case because the high school had no history with that university. The counselor also gave Ben the email address for the admissions officer, and gave the admission officer Ben's contact, as well.

I think this series of events serves as a perfect example of the power that comes from multiple mentors working together to support a young person, ultimately empowering Ben to advocate for himself.

Q: Does my child really need the school counselor's help?

The answer to this is a resounding YES!

Aside from the student themselves, the school counselor is the person most important to a college application. That's because they act as the administrative bridge between the student, the high school, and the university.

Now, it's true that not every student is going to need help with the application itself, or want the counselor to look over their admissions essays. But if nothing else, they are going to need their counselor to forward their transcript and fill out a School Report. Most likely, they'll also want to get a recommendation letter and to enlist their counselor's support in obtaining recommendations from their teachers. Therefore, even if your child doesn't need or want advice, their school counselor is still going to play a central role.

In fact, there are multiple parts to a counselor's involvement with the application process. To begin with, and as I've mentioned before, the school counselor is an important source of information. They know the admissions requirements and deadlines back to front, but they also have an awareness of admissions trends. Through programs like Naviance or MaiaLearning, school counselors have access to data that many students and parents cannot otherwise know. They can see graphs showing the distribution of where students have applied in past years, where they've been admitted, rejected, waitlisted, and whether these results have been during the early decision, early action, or regular decision periods. This can be invaluable for any student.

Let's imagine a student, Luna, wants to apply for early decision but is very torn between three schools: School A, School B, and School C. Early decision is a binding process, so when one applies, they are committing to go to that school if accepted. And because of the binding nature of the application, a student cannot apply to more than one at a time. All three schools have great programs and are a great fit for Luna's interests and lifestyle, both as a student and as a person. She can't decide, so she goes to speak to her school counselor and lays out her dilemma. From there, the counselor pulls up the high school's trend profile. Together, they find out that in the past five years Luna's high school has had 20 people apply to each of the three colleges she's considering. In that time, one person got into School A, zero people got into School B, and six people got into School C.

All other things being equal, a student like Luna can take that data and see that School C, for whatever reason, has a stronger history of admitting students that had similar profiles and applications to hers, so it makes statistical sense for her to choose School C for early decision. And the data that helps her decide this is something she wouldn't have known to look for- nor had access to- without the school counselor.

Once a student has settled on the schools to which they are excited to apply and, ultimately, attend, the counselor can connect them with people at that school. Typically, an admissions officer at a college is going to be responsible for recruitment for a specific region, so they'll be in regular contact with counselors from schools in that region. Depending on where your child is applying, their counselor might have pre-existing contacts within those admissions offices (from hosting university visits or helping organize college fairs, for example). If they don't, there are processes in place for them to easily get in touch; hearing from a school counselor is something that an admissions officer at any university would expect and accept. This can be a great way for your student to learn more about the school through personal contact, get put onto a mailing list about upcoming events (both virtual and on-campus), and generally get a leg-up on their process by making their name known at a school prior to even applying.

However, perhaps the most crucial role that a school counselor plays in the admissions process is by helping corroborate details and providing context for what a student puts in their application. They do this in two ways: first, with letters of recommendation and second, with the School Report.

A student will often need multiple letters of recommendation for their application (there are some wonderful institutions which don't require this, namely some of the largest public schools in the U.S). These letters don't just show a student is well-liked by their teachers or the administration, rather they serve as an important tool for the college to confirm details. For instance, if a student says that they founded a club or played on a school team, the admissions office expects there to be some mention of these activities in the recommendation letters. If the student's counselor or teachers don't mention anything similar, the admissions officer reading the application might have a hard time believing the student, or at least think they're exaggerating their involvement.

Part of a counselor's job is to understand the kinds of details admissions officers are looking for. They know how to write a recommendation that frames the student in the best light. And what's more, they can help teachers do the same in their letters of recommendation!

A new teacher being asked for a recommendation may not have a good idea of what to write, so they'll repeat what the admissions officer already knows: "This student has performed really well"; "They've achieved good grades in my class"; "They turn in all their assignments on time." The admissions officer can infer these things from the student's transcript. The things they want to know are qualitative: How does the student participate in class? Are they kind and helpful to their classmates? These are the kinds of person-centered questions they're asking. A counselor can prompt a teacher to include such assessments in their letter.

The counselor may also have knowledge about a student's life that can help flesh out a recommendation and paint a more complete portrait of the student. For example, they may know that the student missed some school for a family emergency and ask the teacher how the student performed at that time. The teacher may then put in their letter, "A year ago in my class, this student had to miss a week of school for a family emergency. I heard from them every day, they checked in with me about what we did in class and asked for any extra notes. They were responsible and thoughtful and, at the time, I didn't even know what they were going through."

These personal touches, the ability to tell a story, are all things a teacher can do that will boost a student's chances of admission. And if they don't know how to do it, the school counselor is the point of contact who can help them develop that skill.

Besides the letters of recommendation, the other way a university will seek more information about a prospective student's application is through the School Report, also known as the Counselor Forms. These are filled out by the counselor and sent along with the transcript, for every single applicant and every one of their applications. The form includes a range of questions about the student, their class load, and the school's curriculum offerings, grading scale, and college preparation history.

The purpose of the School Report is to put the student's grades and achievements in context, which helps admissions officer understand the relative academic rigor of the student's chosen course load. Admissions officers get applications from all over the country, so they aren't necessarily going to know anything about the school a student is applying from, how many students there are, how grades are determined, or how many students from that school typically go onto 2 or 4-year universities. Without this information, the transcript is significantly less helpful for assessing a student.

For example, if a student is applying with straight A's, the admissions officer is going to want to know if that student is taking the most difficult classes at their high school. If a school offers International Baccalaureate (IB) curriculum or Advanced Placement (AP) classes, for example, but the student isn't taking any, the fact that they're getting straight A's becomes less impressive. If anything, it signals to the university that the student isn't willing to challenge themselves academically. On the other hand, if a school doesn't have IB or AP classes and the student is taking the hardest classes available to them, and doing very well, the university wants to know that, also. The School Report is how they obtain this information.

I've said this before and I'll continue saying this throughout this book: the more mentors a young person has, the better. If your child's school has a school counselor on staff, it's never a bad idea for your student to reach out to them, and the more they can do so throughout the application process (and even before) the better.

With the increasingly large number of people applying to each college and university every year, students can get frustrated and discouraged when trying to stand out from the pack. School counselors are an important resource, excellent advocates, and absolute allies for any student who wants to make sure that they aren't lost in the shuffle. Universities look to school counselors as an authority on the full, complex picture of the students in their care. The better a counselor knows a student, the better they will be at communicating that student's full story to others.

Your teen will have the most success if their relationship with their school counselor is approached with understanding, compassion, and an attitude of collaboration.

But what if my child is having trouble getting an appointment?

Here's the unfortunate reality: school counselors are ALL overworked. Every year their responsibilities expand; every year students need more support; every year counselors are faced with greater demands. Counselors do their best with the resources available, but it's possible for things to slip through the cracks ... if students do not play an active role in this relationship.

Of course, that doesn't mean that you shouldn't expect help or support for your teen. Every teenager needs- and deserves- support! But it does mean that your teen will have the most success if their relationship with their school counselor is approached with understanding, compassion, and an attitude of collaboration. Remember, the counselor's job isn't to do things for their students, it is to enable students to do things for themselves. The more prepared a student is when reaching out to their counselor, the easier it will be for the counselor to help them in-turn.

I've had many conversations where I've asked school counselor friends of mine about a certain mentee, only to have them tell me that they "just don't ever hear from" that student. Ever. At all. As I explained above, this is a real concern, not least because the counselor is responsible for answering a host of questions about the student's overall character and traits in the letter of recommendation and in the School Report. If a student has never reached out to their counselor, the counselor doesn't have much to go on. In turn, the admissions officer will be left with very little information or understanding of the applicant and may well assume that the student did not show initiative in their application process.

In college and university, a student will have to ask questions, build connections, and seek advice and support. Their relationship with their high school counselor can be a great way to build up these skills and habits. It's vital that students recognize that most of what counselors do outside the very basic is often done on their own time and outside of the strict bounds of what is expected of their job. Counselors are passionate about working with young people. They want to help! But like all school administrators, they often get caught up in putting out the daily fires that arise. They may not always follow up or chase down students to discuss ways they can strengthen their college application, so students will have to be proactive.

Let's brainstorm some steps that a student can take to get support from their school counselor. Start with an email:

Hi [Insert School Counselor's Title and Name],

I hope you're having a good week!

I'm sure you're very busy this time of year but I could really use some advice regarding (insert topic here: summer planning; courses for next year; discussing potential teacher recommenders; brainstorming colleges, etc.) Would it be possible for me to come in for a meeting? I'd be happy to come in whenever is most convenient for you, even if it's just for five minutes.

In the meantime, if there's anything else you need from me, or anything I could do to prepare ahead of time, please let me know. I'd love your support and expertise in this. Thanks so much. I hope to hear back from you soon.
Thank you again.

Sincerely,
[Full Name (Insert graduating class year here for additional context.)]

Hopefully, this is all it takes, but we all know that emails can get buried very quickly. If your student doesn't hear within a week or so, it's time to send a follow-up in the same email thread. Be polite. Don't assign blame. Reiterate the request. Something like this:

Hi again!

Sorry to bother you again, I just wanted to double check that you received my last email. As I said, I'd really appreciate some of your time when you can spare it. Thank you so much and I hope to meet up soon.

Thank you,
[Full Name]

At this point, most counselors will make sure to get back to the student. But obviously there is always the possibility that a student will try everything in their power to schedule some time with their counselor and still never get a response. Some counselors just don't have the time, don't think they have the time, or simply don't believe their help is needed in that particular situation (especially if it's a student in the 9th or 10th grades). In many public high schools, especially, where most students often apply to in-state colleges or universities, a letter of recommendation from the college counselor isn't necessary. Therefore, the counselor just needs to answer a series of questions about the school and the student's transcript, meaning to do their job, they don't have to know each specific student well.

In these cases, it's true that a counselor might not feel the need to take time to meet personally with their counselees. However, there are always going to be situations where a student needs basic guidance from an informed professional, and a school college counselor is vital when this happens. So, what do we do?

At this point, it's completely fair for a parent or guardian to reach out to the college counselor and request the meeting on behalf of the student. Oftentimes, a school official will respond to an email or phone call from parents/guardians requesting a meeting, even when the student has asked several times with no response. Yes, this illustrates a greater flaw in our society's overall approach to teenagers, and our dismissal of their needs and voices. But sadly, it may happen, and that's just life. Try not to be too frustrated about it (or let your student get too frustrated about it). Just step in to support them and get that meeting. And when you do, I still (highly) recommend entering it with a sense of gratitude for the counselor's time and expertise.

If you try all of this and still hit some roadblocks, I recommend going to another administrator to find an advocate who can help your family work with the counselor. And in some very unusual cases, I have encouraged students to get other administrators or a head of a department to fill out the counselor recommendation portions of their application instead of the designated college counselor. Colleges and universities allow this as long as the person filling out the form has access to behavioral, academic, and some personal history of the student. This portion of the application is most often referred to as the "Counselor Forms" but in reality, they are the "Counselor/Administrator Forms" and they can be completed by any official at the school who knows the student-applicant outside of simply teaching them in a class.

Please note, the last few suggestions really are for outlier scenarios. Chances are with a little patience, and maybe some persistence, your teen should be able to get an appointment.

Your student doesn't need to wait until they need something specific to start building a positive relationship with their counselor. Encourage them to swing by their counselor's office from time to time to say "hello", or "hi" when they see their counselor around campus. Kindness matters. For a counselor who is overworked and constantly having demands made of them, a kind word from a student can be a great remind-er for why they got into this field in the first place: they wanted to help young people. Sometimes that's all it takes to remind them of the grati-tude and exhilaration they experience when helping a thoughtful young person think about- and plan- their future.

As the parent, you can also model this for your child. When reaching out to the counselor yourself, be polite (always say "please" and "thank you"). If your student meets with their counselor, send them an email:

Hello,

[I/We] just want to sincerely thank you for taking the time to meet with [Student]. They really appreciate all your support, and [I/we do], too.

Hope you have a great rest of your week.

Thank you,
[Parent/Guardian]

Simple gestures like this can go a long way with a counselor. You're not asking them for anything here, but if you have to in the future, they will remember that you have always gone out of your way to show your ap-preciation.

The same principles apply for any direct communication you have with your student's counselor. For example, if you receive a personal email from the counselor or administration about something your stu-dent needs to do, or has not yet completed, "reply all" and copy your student, too. Respond something like this:

Thank you for the heads up. I'm copying [Student] on this email, also. I know they'll make sure to get this (whatever the information or answer is) to you ASAP. Please don't hesitate to reach out if anything else comes up!

Thank you again for your support and the continued communication.

Best,
[Parent/Guardian]

Discuss expectations with your student. Let them know that the school counselor is there to help and support them, and that you are there to help and support them, but that they need to ask and communicate clearly when they want or need support. Learning to ask for help and navigate these dynamics with the adults in their life is part of a teenager's process of individuation, of growing up. It's how they develop their own self-awareness. It's how they learn to manage their own time.

Let them know that it's always okay to say, "I don't know", "I need some help", or "I would appreciate some advice." In turn, we must hope that the adults in their life will be truly supportive and kind. Most are. Keep encouraging your student to reach out to those educators and mentors who lift them up. Make sure to thank those adults who make a difference for your student. As for your communication with your teen, "I'm so proud of you" often goes a long way.

Q: When is the right time to hire a private advisor?

There is no single, universal, one-size-fits-all, "right" time to hire a private advisor. While most families who do hire an IEC, do so when the student is beginning 12th grade, others reach out earlier, in 11th or late 10th. Some even begin prior to that. There can certainly be benefits to reaching out to a private college advisor sooner, but the "right time" is subjective, and it's going to change from person-to-person and family-to-family.

The right time for your student is going to depend on your answer to these two questions:

1. Is your teen thinking a lot about- and getting stressed by- the idea of college applications?
2. What are you looking to achieve by hiring a private advisor?

I know from experience that a lot of parents start worrying about the college application process very early on. But for a young person in their second year (of a traditional, U.S., four-year high school), the college application process is as far away from them as eighth grade is, just in the other direction, and that probably feels very distant. That's because it *is*. This doesn't mean it's not okay to plan or brainstorm, have a sounding board or offer some perspective. *It's that as a private advisor, I don't want to come into a situation where a student isn't stressed and create that stress by forcing them to focus on aspects of their future that are so abstract, when they simply don't need to be thinking about them yet.*

Now, when the student starts to have concerns themselves, when they begin worrying about what they should prioritize or asking questions about university programs and career paths they're considering, that's a situation where it can be helpful to bring in an outside expert.

If a parent is looking to hire an advisor for a freshman or sophomore, they need to have reasonable expectations. The goal early on is not to get the student admitted into a specific school, or to get a jump on the application process. No tangible outcome can be achieved at that point in time. Instead, the advisor's goal is to establish trust with the student, support them through their stress, encourage them to start asking thoughtful questions, and build their confidence. The student needs to know that there's somebody who will take the time to listen to their concerns and provide thoughtful, informed answers. They need to know that their questions and concerns are valid and won't fall by the wayside.

For some students, their private advisor is the first person to challenge them to articulate the many pieces of themselves. These conversations might be the first time they've spoken out loud about the things they're most worried about, that are most authentic to them, that they're most unhappy with, or that they want to work on. It might be the first time they've really taken an accounting of their own strengths and weaknesses. Building a clearer understanding of themselves not only helps them choose a path that really works, but it gives them the confidence to walk that path and to advocate for themselves along the way.

> **For some students, their private advisor is the first person to challenge them to articulate the many pieces of themselves.**

Students entering university need to feel comfortable approaching adults, asking them questions, and seeking out guidance and mentorship on their own. If they can't bring themselves to make connections, their time at school will be limited to the confines of their textbooks and lecture notes. Not that these things aren't important, but it's the relationships formed at school that make the university experience invaluable. To hire a private advisor early can instill the confidence and encourage the independence needed for a student to succeed as they transition from high school to university.

The other potential benefit of hiring a private advisor early on is to make sure that everyone, both the student and their family, is informed and on the same page as the process proceeds. What I have found in my two-plus decades as an advisor is that there a lot of common misconceptions about college and university that both parents and students absorb without ever realizing it, which can lead to a nasty shock when what someone thinks they know runs up against the truth.

Several years ago, one of the families I'd been working with, remotely, asked me to fly to Miami to speak with them and their son, in-person. When I arrived, we all sat down together and the student I'd been working with proudly told me that he'd decided to study business at Harvard and Stanford. This, of course, sounds like a very laudable and ambitious plan! The only problem is that it was also impossible. Undergraduate business programs do not exist at Harvard or Stanford.

The boy's father was not pleased when I pointed this out: "What are you talking about? I've hired dozens of people who studied business at Harvard and Stanford." And I had to explain that yes, it was very likely that he'd hired people with *Master's* in Business Administration (MBA's) from Harvard Business School or the Graduate School of Business at Stanford, but neither university has an undergraduate business degree available.

I use this example because, by the time this family came to me, they'd already developed so many misconceptions, and these had become part of their family narrative and expectations. Universities are complex institutions, and there are so many of them. It can be almost impossible to begin to discern one from the other, let alone nuances of specific programs. People don't want to realize how much incorrect information circulates around them, or how easy it is to latch on to something inaccurate. It can be very hard to unlearn our own assumptions when we think we already know something.

Every year people apply to the University of Chicago, knowing only that it's a good (great, unique, wonky) school, intending to study engineering, perhaps only to find out later (in their rejection letter, perhaps) that the University of Chicago doesn't have an engineering program. This shouldn't be happening. A private advisor can help you identify and correct these kinds of knowledge gaps and misconceptions before they derail your child's application process.

Ultimately, individual needs are going to be different, especially in this process which is creative and qualitative. This is why speaking to a private advisor would be most beneficial. As I mentioned before, many families hire a private college advisor solely during the college application process. In that situation, the parents just want someone with professional knowledge to answer questions and refine their child's application, so the student's relationship with their advisor has a more limited scope. That's perfectly reasonable. Personally, I think advisors do their best work when they are given the opportunity to get to know a student and establish a real partnership. It's through the mentor relationship that a private advisor can really help the family with the whole cycle of emotions and expectations that come with college applications to get the student ready for the transition ahead, to a university that fits all their academic, social, and developmental needs while also fitting the family's budget. Trustworthy relationships, however, take a longer time to build.

Q: How do I find the right private college advisor for my child?

In a sense, this is two separate questions: "How do I find a college advisor?" and "How do I know that advisor is the right fit for our family?" They're both important questions, so I'm going to take some time to answer both fully.

First off, how do you find a private college advisor?

You should know that college counseling is not a super regulated industry—one does not need specific training or certification to call themselves a private college advisor. However, that isn't necessarily a bad or scary thing. There are lots of smart, capable, compassionate people out there who really love working with young people, and you certainly don't need to be a certified professional to be a good mentor. It all depends on what your family is looking for—someone who is a member of a professional organization could end up being a bad fit, and someone with no membership in any organizations could be excellent.

When starting the search for a private college advisor, it doesn't hurt to start close to home. Approach your teen's school counselor (or another administrator or teacher at their school) and ask if they have any recommendations for people they've worked with. This is an ideal scenario, especially if the school counselor has an existing relationship with your student, because they'll hopefully be able to recommend someone that they not only trust but also think would be a good fit.

Make sure you approach the request delicately. Some school counselors won't respond well to being asked because they think of private advisors as encroaching on their territory. But in the vast majority of cases, the school counselor will understand that this is something the family wants for some extra peace of mind, and they'll be eager to recommend someone that they know will be a positive force in the student's life (not to mention someone with whom they can easily work).

If none of the staff at your child's school can recommend anyone, try expanding your search to other people in your community. Ask some parents, or even some of the students at your child's school if they've worked with anyone that they liked. And if you can't get a recommendation from someone you trust, or if you're really set on only hiring a professional, there are a couple of professional development organizations out there that have regional lists of advisor who have membership within those organizations.

- https://www.internationalacac.org/member-directory-#/
- https://www.iecaonline.com/quick-links/member-directory/

Your teen's advisor also doesn't need to be a private advisor for hire. Many families don't have the resources or even the interest in this more formal arrangement. Instead, they'll look to someone who's already a role model in their child's life, a trusted mentor amongst their friends or other parents. It could be a tutor or a coach that the student really likes.

Sometimes, a private college advisor can just be someone who's willing to be an extra pair of eyes on essays and applications, someone who can come in and help your teen and your family communicate and set your expectations with one another. If you're unsure about hiring someone for whatever reason, consider just finding someone that your child likes and can talk to, and go from there.

Which brings me to the second part of this question: how you know that a private advisor is the right one for your family. I'll admit I take a different approach to this than many might.

The truth is that while yes, parents are paying for this service, the relationship and the trust ultimately needs to be built between the student and the advisor. In my opinion, the student feeling comfortable with the adult a family hires is going to be the most important part of the fit. Whether or not a private college advisor is helpful largely depends on whether the student can be honest about what they're encountering, thinking, and feeling as they go through this process. If a student doesn't like their advisor, the experience will likely be a waste of time. Personally, I believe the student should get a lot of input as to who a family selects.

Many families go into this arrangement wanting something very regimented and tangible from a advisor. For example, they want the advisor to meet with their teen "every week at a specific time", talk to them about a laundry list of items, and then send the parents a report that lays out exactly what they talked about and what they're planning to cover the following week. This type of helicopter parenting is not for me and, frankly, it's not really for any teen I've ever met either.

Don't get me wrong, this works for some families. But in my experience, it can also shift the nature of the student-advisor relationship from one that is taking stress *off* the student, to one that is putting more responsibility and worry upon them. Your student shouldn't feel like their college advisor is there to surveil them or supervise them while they do what their parents want them to.

I want my students to feel like they're taking ownership of their own future, and that I'm an ally for them through this. I want them to feel like they can ask me for help when tackling the things that are stressful for them, so they can free up time and energy to pursue the things they love. Young people have so many responsibilities. They work harder, they're dealing with more information and input than any generation before them, and the ideas of "success" are increasingly narrow. I never want to feel like I'm adding on to the challenges or stressors of my mentees.

If you're unsure about hiring someone for whatever reason, consider just finding someone that your child likes and can talk to, and go from there.

Instead, I think of my role as that of an advocate for the student with whom I'm working. And again, to be effective at this, the student should want to communicate with me. A parent might think that I'm the best advisor in the world, because they heard that from a friend of a friend, but if their child doesn't want to talk to me and doesn't want to work with me, it won't matter what the parents think. The parents might be the ones paying for this service, but trust has to be between the teen and the advisor.

This may make some parents uncomfortable, but a really good advisor is sometimes going to need to mediate and to set boundaries for the family, alongside the young person. Sometimes I have to step in and say, "I know you don't want to hear this, but it's not necessary to be working on that part of the plan right now. It would be more beneficial if we put energy into X, Y, and Z."

Parents care so much about their kids, but sometimes the way this gets expressed is through catastrophizing. They worry: their teen doesn't have enough community service; they're not in any sports; they don't play music anymore. It's often a lot of negative ideas, and this can become projected onto the advisor when that relationship is established.

A good advisor can resist arguing and just stay the course and defend the student's time and attention. Oftentimes, parents want to fill up the student's schedule with more commitments, but more isn't necessarily better. Sometimes more is just ... more.

Just a few weeks ago, I had a concerned mother approach me after I gave a talk to a group of parents and counselors. She explained to me that her son was a high school freshman who played water polo. She said that "he loved it so much" and "it was his happy place", but that it also took up too much time, in her opinion. She asked me, "He's a freshman now, but starting in 11th grade, he's going to have to start taking harder classes. When should he give up water polo? Should I have him just stop right before 11th grade or should he stop earlier?"

A good private advisor can help them achieve this sense of confidence, through mentorship, if everyone involved, especially the teen, trusts the advisor to do their job.

To me, this is emblematic of the way parents overthink this process. We have a student whose happiness, relationships, mental health, and wellness all stem from this one activity, water polo. And yet, the parent who is so worried about academics that she wants her son to quit the thing that brings him the most happiness, in favor of putting more on his "plate of responsibilities", adding even more stress, while also taking away the activity that most helps him deal with that stress. This is a false equivalence that parents sometimes fall prey to, requiring their students to make choices between two things that are not similar.

In a situation like this, a good private advisor will help the family understand first, we don't have to plan for this right now. This is in the future; we can decide that when it comes time. But secondly, when we get to that moment in time, why don't we try to see if it's something that's doable? People have managed to do both, a sport and school, at the same time, even at his school. Let's see what he's able to do and make a choice as he grows through this. Most importantly, let's make sure the student is part of this conversation, rather than mandating that he must give up this thing he loves in order to focus on his academics, which he's already doing very well.

The right private advisor, someone who can really make a difference in your student's life, may in fact end up setting boundaries with you. That's a good thing! You're hiring this person to act in the best interest of your student. The ultimate goal of this process is for your teen to be self-sufficient, to have confidence and a sense of independence that they can take into this next stage of their life. A good private advisor can help them achieve this sense of confidence, through mentorship, if everyone involved, especially the teen, trusts the advisor to do their job.

PART TWO

Quick Facts: Universities and Colleges

Over the course of my work, I have seen firsthand how many misconceptions are circulating about the higher education system in the United States. These misconceptions are not only frustrating to hear, they're also potentially detrimental to young people's education and futures. If you're making decisions based on wrong or incomplete information, it's easy to end up on the wrong path and not realize it until it is far too late.

That's what this section of the book is for: to tackle some of the common concerns and questions I've heard from students and their families regarding universities and colleges, and hopefully to enable teens and families to make informed decisions about their higher education pursuits.

Q: How does the U.S. system differ from other systems of higher education?

Before we take a look at some other higher education systems, we should first lay out how the university system functions in the United States. What is a university?

A university is an institution made up of more than one college. Colleges are smaller educational units which have a singular subject focus or a much narrower subject focus, such as the College of Arts and Sciences, the College of Engineering, or the College of Business. Colleges operate independently within the University, and generally have their own facilities, buildings, and administration. Not every college is going to offer undergrad programs, and some will offer both undergraduate and graduate courses.

Taking Columbia University as an example, Columbia is the umbrella under which there are 21 different colleges, including a College of Medicine, a College of Journalism, a College of Law, etc. Of those 21 colleges, only three are undergraduate-focused, bachelor's degree colleges. This tells us some things about the general scope, focus, and population of the university. We expect the university to be research-heavy and for the majority of the student body to be pursuing graduate studies (as opposed to undergraduate- or bachelor's- degrees).

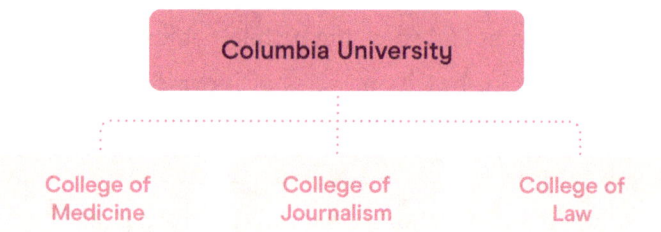

This also illustrates the difference between a university and a college (i.e. liberal arts college) or other types of independent private colleges, such as Babson College, a private business school in Massachusetts, or Wellesley College, an all-women's, liberal arts-focused college just down the street from Babson. These colleges aren't under a university umbrella but function similarly to those which are, schools with a single focus (liberal arts; engineering; business; health sciences) or at least a narrower focus in a specific field or range of fields. While they may offer graduate studies, most focus primarily- or entirely- on undergraduate courses.

Admission in nearly every other country's system of higher education is very narrow.

Now, the difference between the U.S. system and most of the other higher education systems around the world comes down to choice and customizability. In the United States, students apply, and are admitted to, the university or the college. In the UK and the rest of Europe, as well to a lesser extent in Canada, students apply, and are admitted to, a single program. So, if you want to go to Georgetown, for instance, you apply to Georgetown University and are accepted to the University, with the chance to take courses across many programs until you find your greatest interest and declare that your "major". But if you want to go Oxford University, you would be applying directly to the one program you are choosing, be it physics, geography, or anthropology, for example. Admission in the U.S. is broad. Admission in nearly every other country's system of higher education is very narrow.

What this means is that students in these countries follow a pre-scribed curriculum. Their classes are picked out for them from the start, and those that aren't must be chosen from lists of program-specific options. There is very little room to branch out, explore other interests, or develop new curiosities, for that matter.

The U.S. system, on the other hand, gives students free reign to decide what their schooling will look like. This schooling can be as generalized, or as focused, as they wish.

If we look at the anatomy of an undergraduate degree, a student in the U.S. will have to take somewhere around 34 classes over the course of their four years (in a semester-based institution). Those classes are divided into three categories: core curriculum, courses within the student's major/concentration, and electives.

There are some requisite courses within these, but all three categories afford students a great deal of room for exploration. Let's take a closer look.

Core curriculum classes, also referred to as "general education" courses or breadth requirements, are a group of courses or course categories that students have to take to graduate, regardless of their major. Most schools will require between six and eight core curriculum courses. For example, a student may need to take an ethics class, a writing class, a science, a social science, an arts class, and a language course to fulfill their core curriculum requirements.

The purpose of a core curriculum is teaching students foundational skills such as critical thinking, problem solving, and effective communication. Universities want every student to be able to speak on scientific principles, they want every student to be able to write a thesis and to be able to communicate their thoughts in writing. They want every student to know how to do effective research and be able to discern whether an information source is trustworthy.

These are important skills for every field of study, and they'll be transferable to any career a student pursues. However, *how* students choose to fulfil their core curriculum requirements and develop these skills is left largely up to each specific student.

The requirements are not meant to constrain a student but, rather, to give them the opportunity to explore their options across multiple departments, try new things, and potentially uncover new interests they've never even considered before. This is how the core curriculum functions—it ensures students get a well-rounded education and become capable learners, without limiting their choices.

This exploration is also facilitated by the amount of choice students have even within a single department. Let's look at English, for example, which students can take to fulfil their humanities or writing requirement(s).

An incoming college freshman might have had four or five English options in their last year of high school, at most. It's very possible that none of those options were very appealing, and that a student might assume they didn't like studying English, in general. But schools like Arizona State, UCLA, the University of Michigan, all of their English departments offer well over 100 courses in a single semester. Even if a student has never had an interest in English, they might get to university and realize that they can take an English class on comedy in film or on the graphic novel. Suddenly, taking a fun class for their core curriculum requirement can develop into a real passion for studying a field they previously believed they disliked.

Now, multiply that experience by the number of subjects that count towards a core curriculum requirement, and then by the number of classes within any of those departments. You can immediately see why core curriculum requirements don't actually offer much in the way of a constraint.

The main part of a student's course load, somewhere between 12-14 classes, will be courses for their specific major, which is a student's main focus or area of study. New students get a year or two before they have to "declare" their major, which just means that they understand they are pursuing this major and what the major requires. Many know what they want to study before even arriving at university, but others don't know, or change their mind along the way.

Once a student has declared their major, they're required to take a certain number of credits or classes within that department. Those courses will have to cover certain requirements. But again, with such a large catalogue of options available, the educational trajectory of any two students, even within the same major, can be vastly different.

Let's say three students start university in the same year, and all three major in economics. The economics major at this university requires students to take 14 courses in the department, but only two courses, micro- and macro- economics, are specific requisites for the degree. The remaining 12 classes are left up to the students, giving them the opportunity to follow their own specific interests and inclinations.

Of the three students, one could choose to focus on development economics, another could be particularly interested in economic downturns and geopolitical crises in Latin America, and the third might be more interested in studying globalization and the world economy. The three classmates could all graduate with an economics degree, having taken almost none of the same classes.

Finally, classes that aren't aimed at the core curriculum or a student's major fall under the umbrella of electives. In our example, where a degree consists of 34 classes, with 8 core curriculum classes and 14 classes going towards a major, a student would be left with 12 courses to use as their electives.

Twelve classes might seem like a lot if you're thinking of electives as a series of unrelated classes, but what electives do is give each student the chance to think about their education, think about their next steps, and decide what they personally want from their university experience.

The possibilities are pretty much endless—really, there are as many different ways to use electives as there are students at any given school.

Some students may use their electives to build on- and further explore- interests outside their major. This is where, for example, you may have a student who took an astronomy class as their science requirement and loved it, so they decide to take the next astronomy class as one of their electives.

Other students might find that they're particularly interested in a single field outside their major. In that case, they may decide to take several classes in that field to obtain a "minor" or even take all 12 elective classes in that field for a "double major".

Still, other students might decide that their electives are best used on a pre-professional program. Pre-professional programs are sets of classes meant to prepare students for graduate studies in law or medicine, for example. To illustrate this idea, let's take an arts major, who plans to go to medical school. To be the most prepared they can be, they would opt to follow their university's pre-med course recommendations, consisting of a biology class, organic and general chemistry classes, a biochemistry class, anatomy, maybe kinesiology, too. At the end of completing the pre-med classes, that student, no matter what their bachelor's degree is in, whether fine art, philosophy, or biology, would be prepared for the first year of medical school.

The point here is that the U.S. system is driven by freedom of choice. Students are given the opportunity to tailor every aspect of their education, from deciding how to fulfil their core curriculum requirements, to settling on a major, to choosing how much to specialize versus how much to explore a broad range of subjects, to deciding the best ways to prepare themselves for the next stage of their life.

Unlike other systems, the U.S. system is major-based, so called because students take the *majority*, not all, of their courses in a single field. Students in the U.S. aren't necessarily expected to use their undergraduate major once they graduate. A student with a bachelor's degree in psychology, for instance, is just as likely to continue on to graduate school or to work as a psychologist as they are to take the transferable skills they learned and apply them while working in marketing, banking, or any number of other "unrelated" fields.

By contrast, programs like those found in the U.K. and the rest of Europe are geared towards career preparedness. The expectation is for students to take their degree and continue on in that field, so classes are geared towards giving them a solid grounding in their area of study. From the beginning, students have a prescriptive and focused schedule, with multiple required classes and any choices limited to a narrow selection of classes within the program. In this system, a student studying economics would be taking almost exclusively economics classes with the end goal of becoming an economist (or taking some other related role).

This isn't necessarily bad—it can be very appealing to students who go to university knowing exactly what it is they want to study and find the amount of choice in the U.S. system to be overwhelming or unnecessary. I see this most with students who are interested in STEM fields, and aren't interested in venturing outside their very specific focus. But for students who really don't know what they want to study, or who have multiple interests and intelligences and want to be able to cast a wide net, and explore multiple options before deciding on an area of study, the U.S. system will give them this opportunity.

At this point I should say that there is one field in the U.S., engineering, which is much more similar to educational systems in the U.K. and the rest of Europe.

Engineering programs are meant to be career training, with the express goal being that engineering students go on to work as engineers. Because of this, engineering programs function more like the career training programs you can find abroad, with a regimented series of prescribed classes every year that are meant to teach students specific job skills that build on themselves over the course of the degree. So, instead of a 14-class major, engineering students can expect for 25-30 classes out of their 34 to be in engineering.

For the most part, this level of broad, holistic education at the undergraduate level is unique in the U.S. system. It is this distinction that's key to understanding the difference between the U.S. system and other schools abroad.

What about cost?

There's one *other* major difference between the U.S. system and other systems abroad: the difference in the cost of tuition.

Students who choose to go abroad to places like Canada, the U.K., and parts of Europe might pay half what students in the U.S. pay, if not even less. I say might because this is by no means a given—depending on the country, the school, and even the program, tuition for international students can be prohibitively expensive, even before accounting for the many expenses inherent to moving abroad.

That being said, there are many less expensive education options around the world. In some countries, education is even free, though it can be difficult to find free English-speaking programs. Other countries, like the Netherlands, Spain, and Italy, have very inexpensive options, even for international students. That's because accessible schooling is considered an important social benefit in these countries. As such, schooling in these places is publicly subsidized.

I don't think I have to tell you that education in the U.S. is very expensive. You can say a lot about why that is (and people certainly do) but one thing to consider is the fact that U.S. schools have invested heavily in hospitality-style features.

In the U.S., students and parents alike expect universities to not only provide for students' intellectual development, but also to prioritize their physical, mental, and emotional health. Features like first-class dorms and cafeterias, well-equipped athletic facilities, and campus green spaces are not optional, but instead are considered an essential part of caring for the overall development and wellness of young people. I can't say that I disagree.

Unfortunately, these kinds of amenities drive up the cost of schooling, which in turn further drives inequality and the inaccessibility of education for many. And in a sort of vicious cycle, these increased costs also inevitably increase students' expectations for schools to justify the cost by providing more amenities.

I think in many ways, we have been primed to think of college as a hospitality industry. This is one of the reasons why some people have a cultural bias against attending their local university. Students want to have this full, immersive experience to "broaden their horizons". They want to go to college somewhere new and exciting and thus, ignore local options that would be much more affordable while providing just as good, if not better, learning opportunities.

> It's important for parents to encourage their children to think of college not as a finish line but rather as a starting point or a next step on the adventure. Education is a lifelong journey!

That's not to say that going to school out-of-state or even abroad should be off the table—like I said, some schools abroad can, in fact, be much cheaper options. But it's important for parents to encourage their children to think of college not as a finish line but rather as a starting point or a next step on the adventure. Education is a lifelong journey! Choosing a school that works for a student's career plans, their interests, their learning style, their budget, their future, that's how that journey gets on the right path.

Q: Should my child be considering rankings when choosing schools?

In my experience, while school rankings can have their place, they can also be actively detrimental to selecting the right university. They should be taken not with a grain of salt but with *the whole saltshaker*.

Let me explain.

Many families turn to the different ranking systems for colleges and universities as a way to become acquainted with institutions they might otherwise have never known. At this most basic level, as a way of getting to know what options exist, these lists can be a useful tool. The problems start when parents and students take the rankings as gospel and treat them as an objective way to compare institutions. They assume that the more highly-ranked a university they choose, the better, and that's frankly just not true.

The first problem with this thinking has to do with methodology.

Let's look at the most well-known university ranking list in the United States, which is compiled by *U.S. News & World Report*. The *U.S. News* scores schools on 17 weighted criteria, covering factors like faculty, graduation rates, retention rates, admissions selectivity, financial resources, among others. A peer assessment of a school's reputation by other universities is another factor, accounting for 20% of the school's final numerical score. The schools are then ranked based on those overall scores.

The data set U.S. News uses when creating their annual rankings is self-reported by the universities. These same universities know that ranking higher will likely mean more applicants, more prestige, and more money. They also know that rising through the ranks naturally with large-scale improvements will require a massive financial investment on their part. As such, they're incentivized to game the system.

In 1996, Richard Freeland took over as president of Northeastern University (NEU). Between low enrollment and massive cuts in funding over the prior decade, he knew that keeping the school afloat would require something drastic. Over the next decade, he led a concentrated effort to raise NEU's place in the U.S. News & World Report university rankings. They reverse-engineered the formula U.S. News was using for their rankings and focused in on select criteria to improve. Naturally, they shot through the ranks.

At first glance, this might seem like a win-win—if the university improves, does it matter *why*? But if you look at the changes Freeland actually made, very few of them had all that much to do with the educational experience or the service provided to students. One change was allowing online applications, which meant the school got more applications, rejected more students, and therefore could report a higher degree of selectiveness in their admissions. Another had to do with boosting their peer review scores. Freeland visited as many universities as possible, schmoozing with the presidents to encourage more, and better, peer review stats for NEU.

When Richard Freeland took over in '96, the school was #162 on *U.S. News'* list. In 2023, nearly 20 years later, it sat at #44. In that sense, the campaign was a rousing success. But it's hard to say how the changes that have been made directly benefit the students. And Northeastern isn't the only one that has prioritized rankings over student satisfaction. It's hard to blame them. When a school's success is intrinsically linked to their rank, why *wouldn't* you game the system or even outright misrepresent your school's data?

But even if we assume the data is unimpeachable, there are larger issues at play.

U.S. News & World Report is not an academic institution nor a non-profit organization—they don't publish their rankings for the benefit of universities or students, they publish them because it's profitable. Thus, everything from the format of the rankings to the data-gathering is geared towards profit as well. It's in their best interest to simplify and flatten nuance as much as possible, to make their list easy to compile and, most importantly, easily digestible for the hungry parents and students who consume it.

This is the real crux of the matter and why these rankings are so deceptive. In order to easily compare schools, organizations like *U.S. News* have to focus on factors that are ... easily comparable, simple to quantify and universal. There's an implication that the schools on the list are all directly equivalent, that a school like Northeastern and another, like Columbia University, essentially offer the same things, just in different cities and to differing levels of "success".

But in reality, Northeastern and Columbia are extraordinarily different from one another. They don't offer all the same programs; they don't have the same campus culture. If you wanted to study environmental engineering, you couldn't do so at Northeastern. If you wanted to major in anything related to business as an undergraduate, Columbia doesn't offer those courses.

Every college or university is going to provide a student with a unique educational experience, and likewise, every student is going to have particular requirements for their college or university. When students focus on the prestige of going to a top-ranked school above all else, they ignore all of the subjective factors that will actually tell them whether that school will be a good fit, factors that can't be quantified or ranked because they're unique to every student.

If tomorrow, Small School X in Central Arkansas were to receive a billion-dollar cash influx from a donor, that money would immediately translate into a higher ranking. That billion plus dollar endowment could boost the school from #200 to #100. For a prospective student, that school would seem to suddenly be better than a hundred more schools, all without anything being functionally different. In fact, the student would know nothing concrete about the benefits of the school from the rankings alone. Nothing about the school's emphasis on teaching, its research, its student-led projects or organizations, its alumni employability. But from their perspective, the school would suddenly be that much more desirable of a destination.

This becomes a vicious cycle. As a school counselor friend often laments, "Every single year we have 85 students applying to the same 15 schools." Students opt for high-ranking schools because of the name recognition, missing out on opportunities at schools that would be a much better fit for their needs. The highly ranked schools reject the majority of these applicants, making themselves appear more selective and boosting their ranking even further.

As those schools ascend in the rankings, the perceived value of their degrees and alumni also increases. Alumni feel more positively about their alma maters and donate more, which again reinforces the rankings. Higher-ranked schools end up ranking higher *because* they're higher ranked. Meanwhile, smaller, less well-funded universities become further obscured.

There are many wonderful small universities across the United States, schools that do some of the best teaching in the country. These schools don't have the donor base or the endowments to compete with larger schools (nor public school resources) in the rankings. They shouldn't have to—they're not trying to provide the same type of service as those larger schools. Forcing them to compete doesn't benefit the schools, nor does it benefit students or prospective students.

Many schools have joined the movement to get rid of the rankings, some going so far as to boycott the rankings by forgoing self-reporting. But for all the schools that protest, there are others that prop up the rankings because they directly benefit from them. Nowhere is this more visible than in the "Ivy League".

We have this myth in the United States, this extremely successful bit of branding that has resulted in a veneration of the Ivy League. The Ivy League is eight schools: Princeton University, Brown University, Columbia University, Cornell University, Dartmouth College, Harvard University, University of Pennsylvania, and Yale University. We think of these schools as the 'best of the best' in the country. These are the schools to which students are supposed to aspire. We've even coined terms like "Little Ivy" or "Public Ivy" to try and capture some reflected glory for universities outside the Ivy League.

But the Ivy League is just an NCAA athletic conference. Like the the SEC or the ACC, the Ivy League is a grouping of eight schools that compete against each other in various sports. And yes, they're all very rich, prestigious universities with a lot of resources and a long history in this country, but they're far from the only schools you can say that about. They're also, again, very different from one another. Dartmouth in the middle of the woods in New Hampshire will have a very different environment and community, a very different type of student, even a different style of teaching than UPenn in the middle of Philadelphia, and both differ from Columbia in New York City.

But the Ivy League is just an NCAA athletic conference.

When we speak of the Ivy League as a single entity, we do the same thing as the rankings—flatten out distinctions, imply that they're all offering the exact same programs, that any of these schools will satisfy any student by sheer virtue of being "Ivy League" schools.

We've projected a degree of aspiration and merit onto the Ivy League that outstrips what you see with other schools. The prestige works directly to the benefit of these eight schools. They have more engaged donor bases, they can charge higher tuition and fees, and they're basically guaranteed to have high-achieving students applying every year. Despite not having an administrative connection to one another, these eight schools rely on their shared reputation to help all of them prosper.

It is unsurprising, then, that Ivy League schools are very invested in perpetuating the Ivy brand.

Ivy League schools do very well in The *U.S. News & World* Report rankings. In fact, the number one spot on the *U.S. News* best national universities list has gone to an Ivy every year since 2001. This isn't unusual—like I said, they're fine schools. But remember, 20% of the score that determines a school's ranking comes from peer feedback, and of course all of the Ivy League schools rate each other very highly because it's good for the shared brand.

None of this is meant to suggest that Ivy League schools aren't actually good, or that the other schools at the top of the rankings aren't actually good. But if your teen is relying on rankings to decide where to apply, they should know they're getting a very skewed perspective on these schools.

There isn't one formula for what makes a school the "best". Rankings can be a useful tool for researching schools, but that's all they are, one single tool. They shouldn't be your starting point, and they *certainly* shouldn't be the only resource to which you turn.

Whether or not you buy into the data that schools use to rank themselves, a higher ranking only matters if you can afford that school. At the end of the day, if a student attends their local university and comes out with a perfect GPA and great relationships with their faculty, they're going to do just fine. They're going to be happier and more successful than those who went out-of-state, spent way over budget, took out too much debt, and ended up struggling from day one after graduating.

I'm going to go into more detail about considerations for choosing a school later on but suffice it to say that the best school for a student is the school that makes the most sense budget-wise, as well as with regard to program offerings. Maybe that school allows a student to live close to home or further away, maybe it's smack dab in the middle of a big city or maybe they're in a sleepy college town.

Ultimately, students need a school which allows them to fully grow into themselves and embrace the identity that they want to create when they go to university. And what that looks like can't be ranked or quantified.

Q: What is a liberal arts degree?

Despite the name, a liberal arts degree doesn't actually mean a degree in the arts. The liberal arts encompass anything that isn't professionally-oriented. That means any major that isn't engineering or undergraduate business is a liberal arts degree. This includes any number of fields within the humanities, but also the social sciences and sciences as well. All of them fall under the liberal arts umbrella.

Ultimately, students need a school which allows them to fully grow into themselves and embrace the identity that they want to create when they go to university. And what that looks like can't be ranked or quantified.

While we're on a roll, let's quickly clear up another misconception. The reason I say that a liberal arts degree is not "professionally-oriented" isn't because the degree isn't useful in a professional setting, but because the skills taught in these classes are not preparing a student for a specific profession. So, a student may end up working in their field of study, and they may even be taking classes or majoring in a subject with a specific profession in mind, but the classes themselves are not meant to be job training.

The liberal arts are not a single path towards a fixed outcome, but instead an educational philosophy that emphasizes a breadth of knowledge and the teaching of transferable skills. Liberal arts programs emphasize problem solving, critical thinking, and effective communication as three principal skills that every student needs regardless of their major. Of course, students will learn a great deal more besides these skills. But no matter what they study, these core competencies will be the foundation of their learning. They'll make use of these skills not only over the course of their university career, but going forward as they join the workforce.

There's an outdated idea I often hear from parents. They want their child to do a "practical" degree and insist that liberal arts degrees would be impractical and can't possibly lead to a job. I hear questions like, "What are they going to do with a philosophy degree?" or "What are they

LIBERAL ARTS

political science

communication

philosophy

music

history

anthropology

art

biology

economics

writing

going to do with an anthropology degree?"

I get it. Older generations have been so focused on single careers throughout their working life. But single careers are simply not how the world functions anymore. Not only do these questions not make sense in today's working world, but they also betray our understanding of what today's jobs look like, and what will and won't make their child "employable".

I get it. Older generations have been so focused on single careers throughout their working life. But single careers are simply not how the world functions anymore.

The truth is, today's job market is *rapidly* changing, and these changes are showing no signs of stopping. By 2030, some of the jobs current college students are considering now won't exist anymore, while others will look completely different from how they do. Some of these students will end up applying for jobs that we don't even have a concept of yet.

How do we train people for a job that doesn't currently exist? Obviously, that's impossible, so we don't try to train students for a specific career. Instead, we train them to be problem solvers, critical thinkers, and effective communicators. In essence, they learn to be excellent learners, which means they can leave university and slot into any field and learn the skills and knowledge they need on the job.

In sports, you hear a lot about the idea of coachability. If you're a talented player with some decent technique, that's a good start, but it isn't all there is. If you're a hard worker that is open to listening and learning, to accepting critique, and to growing as a player, you can join a team and a great coach can help you become truly great in your sport. But if you don't have the willingness to learn, it doesn't matter how great the coach is, or how naturally talented a player may be. One will not be able to learn, or adapt to, the skills that are required. Over time that person will fall behind.

Coachability is the number one skill that will serve today's students in tomorrow's highly dynamic job market. It's also the basis of a liberal arts degree.

Even if we limit our decision to the job market as it is now, I think a lot of parents would be extremely surprised by how little a student's degree matters to the career that chooses them. Whether we're talking about working in banking, or in consulting, starting a business, or working in tech, they're just as likely to hire somebody who studied art history as somebody who studied philosophy or economics, because a candidate from any of these backgrounds will have the same core competencies (critical thinking, problem solving, effective communication) as a result of their liberal arts education.

In terms of their value to an employer, a philosophy degree, an art history degree, and an economics degree have equal weight. Just consider, what are you doing in these classes? You're reading material, you're researching, you're having discussions, you're asking questions, you're consolidating your thoughts into writing. You're learning to be thoughtful and process information in different ways and then apply it, analyze it, and express it. These are the soft skills that are valued in the job market.

And yes, most jobs will require a certain amount of industry knowledge. It's pretty obvious that if you're working at an art gallery, you're going to need knowledge about art. An art history degree may give you a leg-up in that respect, but you don't necessarily have to have that knowledge going in.

If somebody with a strong liberal arts background wants to work in a gallery, they can learn on the job. They know how to research and how to ask the right questions and they're going to be very coachable within their new field. Even without an art history degree, a candidate may have other work experience or knowledge that makes them more desirable than someone *with* said degree. And this same principle applies to many jobs today.

Employers don't need you to know everything about an industry—they only need you to be a quick learner who can easily adapt to a new field. This isn't conjecture. There is research to back it up. Plus, I've seen it for the past twenty years with just my own students. I've had students who did not study art history, nor art, but ended up working in galleries; equally so, I have had students who studied fashion or design who went on to work in consulting or in finance, because they could easily pick up the skills they needed.

Coachability is the number one skill that will serve today's students in tomorrow's highly dynamic job market. It's also the basis of a liberal arts degree.

So, does the degree really matter? I'd say the person matters more. If a student is interested in history but majors in economics because their parents are telling them it's a "practical" degree, that could end up being a big mistake. Because, of course, economics is also a liberal arts degree. It's a theory-based degree with lots of reading that teaches those same foundational skills as history (say it with me: problem solving, critical thinking, and effective communication!) But the student who majors in a subject that resonates with them will likely be happier, learn more, and produce better work than a student who goes into a field just because they think it has more practical value.

A "practical" degree isn't practical if a student isn't motivated. If they do poorly, don't gel with the material, and can't really make it stick in their mind, they're learning little. A student with exceptional grades in history will probably go a lot further than a student with middling or poor grades in economics, in part because they will be much stronger in those transferable skills we've been discussing. Just in terms of caring for the emotional and mental well-being of young people, there is absolutely an intrinsic value in studying a subject that we find interesting, motivating, and that is fundamentally pleasurable for us to learn.

As I keep emphasizing, this is the basic value of a liberal arts degree—it gives each student the opportunity to discover what resonates *for them*. That may be history, it may be economics, it may be chemistry. The important thing is giving those students the space to figure it out for themselves, and trusting in the fact that any field they choose will be able to prepare them for the dynamic and changeable job market they will face on the other end.

Q: Is it better for my child to pick a major or be undeclared when applying?

As we've already discussed, the first year or two of university is a time for students to explore and try different things. That being the case, your teen is very unlikely to be asked to, or expected to, declare a major when they're applying to schools! It's not so much that there's a better or worse way to do it, there just probably won't be an option unless you're applying to a handful of very specific programs.

This isn't to say your teen shouldn't start thinking about their interests and considering potential majors now. While they won't be applying directly to a major, students will be asked to indicate "areas of interest" on their university application. This is a time for them to think broadly.

Schools want to accept well-rounded, intellectually curious individuals who have multiple potential study interests. This isn't just about accepting a specific type of learner but also about the universities making sure that all programs have incoming students.

Universities know that many students are going to change their mind, or change their indicated major over the course of their degrees. But they also can't have every single student studying economics, biology, or political science. They need to make sure that they have students who are interested in psychology, in history, in literature, because of course these departments exist and need students as well.

When filling out college applications, students should take the opportunity to really imagine multiple future paths for themselves. It's a model that takes some of the pressure off what is already a stressful situation—students don't need to be anxious about making the "wrong" choice because they're not selecting a major they're going to be stuck with, just indicating their interests. No one is going to hold them to what they said if they get to university and decide to pursue something new or unexpected. In fact, it's very much the opposite: universities want students to take the time to dance around different programs, try new things, and only then select the major that makes the most sense for them.

There are a handful of exceptions (or semi-exceptions) to this rule, where students will need to be slightly more strategic with their applications. Specifically, engineering programs, undergraduate business programs, and music & fine arts programs.

If a student is considering an undergraduate degree in either engineering or business, they should be using that interest as their primary filter through the college application process. For one thing, not every university offers these majors, and of those which do, many require students to apply directly to the business college or college of engineering. These programs also often have strict high school prerequisites, like calculus or higher-level sciences, which mean students need to plan ahead to make sure they're eligible. Plus, most schools make it very difficult to transfer into the college of engineering after starting a major in another program that is outside of that university's college of engineering. Put together, this all means that students interested in business or engineering programs will need to commit ahead of time, at least to understanding the requirements for their desired program(s).

A student can always change their mind later, but transferring out of these programs (engineering or business) is going to be a lot easier than trying to get into them after already starting. In other words, to change one's major from chemical engineering to chemistry is MUCH less chal-

Students don't need to be anxious about making the "wrong" choice because they're not selecting a major they're going to be stuck with, just indicating their interests.

lenging than moving from chemistry to chemical engineering. For that reason alone, students with the capacity for- and interest in- these courses should, as I said, use that interest as their primary filter.

Even within engineering, students are not likely to be asked to declare a *specific* major when applying. Most universities offer a first-year experience-type of course for all declared engineering freshmen, that exposes students to all the types of engineering the university offers before asking them to declare a major. So, while they will need to decide to apply to the college of engineering ahead of time, they won't be expected to know exactly which discipline within engineering they're going to study.

The other exception is, of course, within music & fine arts, any programs that are portfolio or audition-based. There are many institutions that allow students to take courses in these programs without majoring in them, but for those who want to major in music, such as vocal or instrumental music, or in painting, drawing, or sculpture, for example, there will be an audition or portfolio process as part of admissions. In these cases, the university will generally review the application first, to make sure the student meets minimum admissions requirements, then pass on the portfolio to the faculty in the desired department, or leave it to the music or theater department to conduct their auditions.

Like engineering and business, music & fine arts programs require planning and commitment ahead of time, both in choosing appropriate schools and programs to apply to and, of course, in preparing a portfolio or audition piece. So yes, in a sense, applying for these programs requires a student to decide their major ahead of time. However, even then, students will still find room for experimentation.

Of course, if you're auditioning as a musician, you're not going to go to the conservatory and suddenly change your focus from opera to flute or guitar. But at a lot of large public institutions, once you're admitted to a specific program within the College of Fine Arts, you then get to take classes across different programs within your first year, before declaring a major. Schools know that their students are coming in with so much creativity, but they might not necessarily have been exposed to all the different potential outlets for that creativity in high school. When they're given the chance to take a film class, an animation class, a design class, a fashion class, a photography class, or more, they may well find a new outlet for their creative energies. And that's possible at many, many schools.

I always encourage my students who are interested in fine arts, music, or theater to go ahead and apply. There are excellent programs out there at schools in almost every state. This includes both public universities and private, arts-focused or conservatory schools. I also don't recommend limiting applications only to private arts schools.

It's likely your public flagship university has a fine arts program. There are great schools that offer conservatories of music, like the Jacobs School of Music at Indiana University or the Eastman School of Music at the University of Rochester. You don't just have to go to Berklee College of Music (although it's also a great place).

With fine arts, as well as with engineering and business, there are schools that have a specific focus on these subjects, but that doesn't necessarily make them the best school for any given student. Attending a school that is just engineering-focused, or just music-focused, is an option, yes. But it all depends on how much interaction a student wants to have with people who are interested in different ideas and problems, or at least goes about understanding the world through a different lens.

At a school like Berklee, where everyone is studying music, students are fully immersed in the culture there, interacting with people who share their passions and interests in the field. Some students might find that ideal, but others might find the lack of interaction with people from different programs and different walks of life stifling. On the other hand, a school like Indiana University offers an array of programs, with students studying across every discipline.

I find that young people want to be around a variety of people. They want to have interesting conversations and expand their worldview, and explore things beyond their personal experiences and interests. These young people are more articulate, more experienced, more skilled, more interested in the world as a whole, and they aren't always satisfied with sticking to the single subject or one skill that they've been working to hone throughout high school.

And actually, to bring it back to choosing a major, that drive to learn and explore is the same instinct that makes the U.S. system, with its opportunities to try multiple things before committing to a single major, so ideal for students. With the incredible amount of choice available, no student ever has to be bored, nor regret their pursuits. At almost every step, they'll have the opportunity to pivot their focus or expand their learning horizons to truly get the most out of their experience.

Q: How should my child go about choosing schools to apply to?

Always start with a budget.

Let's just caveat this section by saying that the financial aid process is absolutely helpful and can really be significant for many, many students. That said, if one's budget is $10,000 per year, looking at $80,000 per year schools because financial aid will come to the rescue, is a really inaccurate hope. That's how we have such tremendous student debt in the U.S., and why the schools continue to increase their costs, because students take enormous financial aid loans to meet their chosen school's costs.

For the family of a young person who's starting the college applications process, helping your child decide on- and apply to- schools is going to require a lot of very honest conversations. The first, and maybe most important, topic to tackle will be money.

It may be uncomfortable, but as parents, your job is to impress upon your student what the budget is, and to emphasize that this is very real. Be honest. It doesn't help anyone if your teen is under the impression that there's a lot of wiggle room, or that financial aid will take care of everything. There is no need to spend time and energy falling in love with a school that's not going to be financially feasible. The sooner everyone gets on the same page about what's realistic, the better.

Any schools where the tuition is entirely outside the budget are easy to eliminate right off the bat. We must also remember that tuition only comprises *part* of the total expense of schooling. Depending on the circumstances, things like food, housing, travel, even entertainment can all end up eating a large chunk of the available budget, too.

These additional expenses can be difficult to estimate, and you'll likely end up going back to the budget multiple times in the process of choosing schools. That being said, make sure you're keeping such costs in mind as you narrow down your options. Most likely, schools where the tuition, alone, comes close to the overall budget, are going to be really tight to afford.

Once the list of potential schools has been narrowed down to the financially realistic options, that's when your teen can start filtering down the list with other factors. The next most important factor is, of course, going to be academics—what programs are available at these schools and what is their reputation in the fields that your student is considering?

As previously discussed, this is where an interest in engineering or undergraduate business is an invaluable understanding. Just as a reminder: not all schools offer these programs and those which do make it much harder to transfer into them from other departments than it is to transfer out. For any student seriously considering these programs, whether or not a university has the program should be a primary filter when deciding where to apply.

If your teen is more interested in a liberal arts focus, their choices open up to many, many institutions across the country. From the many, small liberal arts colleges, to the larger, public universities in your state. At this point, the pool of potential schools may still be quite big, so you should encourage your student to look closer at the specific programs in which they're interested.

Of course, a student's intended major may well change over the course of their actual degree! Still, if they're really interested in a single field of study when applying for schools, then looking for universities that are known to have strong programs in that particular subject can be a good way to narrow options, as well.

After identifying budget and programs, there are other filters that I find helpful. Some may read this and disregarded what I'm about to say as inconsequential, but the truth is that I see the difference such qualities have made in thousands of lives over the years. These are aspects of lifestyle, interests, and values, considerations that are less concrete or practical, but will likely have a huge impact on a student's happiness and wellbeing.

For example, if a student is really outdoorsy and loves to camp and hike and be in nature, they probably don't want to go to school in a busy urban area that's miles and miles away from the nearest tree. A student who does a sport like surfing would probably be happiest near the ocean, but a snowboarder likely wants to be somewhere mountainous with heavy winters.

The important factors are going to change depending on the student, but it's important for each young person in this position to think about, and define, what they value most. Maybe they badly want to be in the city, or maybe they get overwhelmed being around too many people. Maybe they want to be really close or really far away from home during the school year. Maybe they're big music lovers and want to live somewhere with concerts and music festivals. Maybe they get sick easily and want to live somewhere temperate. Maybe they're a vegetarian and want to make sure they'll have food options nearby. All of these considerations could have a real impact on a young person's quality of life during their college years.

You might already be seeing how the budget comes back into consideration at this point, as well. The environment, lifestyle, and campus experience a student is looking for can have a drastic effect on their budget. Going to school in a city typically comes with a much higher cost of living, for example, especially if the school doesn't have housing guarantees for students. A really remote location might mean the student really needs transportation, which comes with its own associated costs.

Speaking of cars, travel is another factor you're going to have to consider amongst all this.

How is your child planning to get to and from school? Are you expecting them to come back for every break? If a student is flying back and forth to start the year, then for Thanksgiving, then winter break, then spring break, and then back home for summer, that's a lot of flights over the course of the school year. If they're driving, the gas costs, and hours spent on the road add up, too. Depending on the school, travelling could get really expensive *and* really disruptive pretty quickly.

There's also monthly spending. Sure, a student *could* never leave the campus and have everything taken care of. They could eat every single meal and find entertainment on campus. Many do and are very happy. But some students want more than that, and they figure this desire into how they choose schools. They have a certain idea of what school will look like, and mean, for them, and it's important to make sure those expectations are in-line with their budget.

PART THREE

The Application Process

The process of applying for university is probably the most complex challenge your teen has ever faced, particularly testing their acute self-awareness. With so many moving parts that require attention over a long timeline, it can be a daunting task.

This chapter is meant as a helpful reference for your teen through the in's and out's of the application process. The hope is to help get the application completed as early as possible while keeping the process smooth and painless.

Q: What is my responsibility as a parent in the process of college applications?

This is going to be hard to hear, but your main role in your child's college applications is probably going to be taking a step back and letting your kid tell you what support they need/want from you.

Yes, you want your child's senior year to be as stress-free as possible. Yes, you want them to be happy and you want to make all of this easier for them. And yes, there will be opportunities for you to provide encouragement and share practical knowledge over the course of this process.

But this is an important transitional moment for your teen. Very soon, they're going to need to know how to move in the world as an adult, how to ask for help, how to advocate for themselves, how to seek mentorship and connections with their professors and other adults. Basically, how to run their own life. Navigating the college application process is a big step in developing the confidence and independence they're going to need to tackle this transition, and wanting to be too actively involved as a parent is only going to derail their progress, as well as their confidence.

While teens do need support and mentorship during their college applications, there is no reason that support needs to be only, or even primarily, from their parents. If anything, I think it's often best for it to *not* be a parent. Partly, that's because you and your teen are going to be stressed out enough as it is. Nagging is not going to make their applica-

8th Grade

Be aware of the courses that you might want to take in high school and find out whether any of these will have pre-requisites that you need to sign up for in 9th grade. If you are able, register for the more rigorous courses in your 9th grade year. If your school is an AP school, maybe take AP Human Geography or AP Psychology, for example. If your school is an IB school, consider whichever math or sciences will allow you to take the appropriate IB math or science classes you may want in 11-12 grades. Otherwise, do your best and read (audiobook) often.

← START

9th Grade

Depending on whether a student has already taken any equivalent to algebra 1 and geometry, they can begin to take the SAT. Do your best in coursework. Begin to explore clubs and activities that excite you, particularly those available IN school and within the community. Introduce yourself to the school counselors and stay in communication with teachers as material becomes more challenging. Register for challenging courses for 10th grade. Read. Write. Listen to podcasts. Learn outside of school.

10th Grade

Continue to be involved in clubs and activities which excite you. Maintain strong grades in rigorous courses. Stay close with teachers. Read and listen to podcasts that teach about things which interest you. Take the SAT. Sign up for rigorous coursework for 11th grade. If you have interest in any specific universities, begin to follow them on social media and go to their admissions websites and sign up for mailing lists. If you're near a university during any sort of trip or vacation, take a quick detour to walk around the campus and explore the community a bit. Over the summer, do something that is learning-focused (reading regularly, learning a language, tutoring younger students, or working a job, for example).

Timeline

11th Grade

Stay focused on grades and coursework. Invest yourself a little bit more in 1-2 of the activities that most excite you. Get your SAT testing done as soon as you can this year, if you haven't already. Begin thinking about the areas of study which are most interesting to you in university, and keep an open mind about how your academic strengths might translate to certain majors in university. Reach out to your school counselor to get their timeline for the months/year ahead. Talk with a few teachers about serving as your recommenders in the college application process. Read. Work. Listen to podcasts. Watch films. Learn outside of the classroom during days off/vacations. Choose rigorous courses for your 12th grade year. Attend any local college/university fairs and introduce yourself to admission officers from schools you have interest in and then follow-up with a thank you email to those counselors you meet or who represent schools you believe are a good fit.

12th Grade

Plan weekends when you can commit a large chunk of time to the creative writing process for the application essays. Maintain grades. Stay active in clubs/activities that you've committed to. Check-in regularly (and thank!) your school counselor and teacher recommenders. Be proud of yourself.

COLLEGE →

tion better. And no parent wants to feel like you have to constantly nag. But the other part of this is that parents often aren't aware of just how much admissions has changed since they went through the whole thing, if they did.

I've heard so many parents say things like, "Well, when I was your age, I just went to the Stanford Dean of Admissions Office and waited until he came out of his office and struck up a conversation and I got in." That's great for those parents, but that's just not the way this works anymore! And it's not helpful for young people to hear that kind of advice. I would argue it's actually the opposite. It's hurtful. It minimizes how much they work and how challenging the landscape of college admissions is now.

So, what *would* be helpful, you ask?

The best thing you can do is make sure your kids have the scaffolding they'll need to make decisions regarding their education. By that, I mean those bits of practical, quantifiable knowledge we've already talked about: the budget, what types of support you can provide, what your expectations are for how far away your child can go, what you think some of their great skills are, a willingness to be a sounding board, not an advice column.

After that, you should be able to ask questions and do so *without judgement*, allowing your teen to set boundaries as they see fit. Ask them: "What are you interested in right now?" "How did you get interested in that?" "Do you think you'd be comfortable talking to that teacher?" "Do you think you'd be comfortable going to your counselor?" "Would it be easier for you if I went with you?" "Would you like to write them an email? I'm happy to look over it if that would be helpful." "Do you have any questions for me?" "Can I be helpful in any way?"

Show them that you're interested in helping but willing to let them take the lead, and then actually follow through in your actions. Being consistent with your words and actions goes a long way with a young person who's dealing with uncertainty, entering this process of discovery, and trying to navigate this and adolescence. They're going to have lots of questions, but they won't say anything if they don't feel safe and unjudged. Reacting defensively or harshly is not going to create an environment where your teen can grapple with the fear and doubt this process brings up.

The other thing parents can, and should, do is encourage and help their teens to seek support and mentorship from other valued adults. These can be family friends, teachers, or coaches. They can also be professionals concerned with admissions, such as school counselors, private advisors, admissions officers. These can also be individuals from non-profit organizations that help students with college applications, such as QuestBridge, PeerForward, and the Posse Foundation.

I really encourage young people to seek out college admissions officers at the universities they're interested in. And I mean specifically the applicants themselves, not the parents. Believe it or not, I'd estimate that over 80 percent of the emails and phone calls that university admissions offices receive are from parents. Don't be that parent!

The reason most admissions officers at universities entered into this field was to work directly with young people, to answer questions and be guideposts for students undergoing this very important transition in their lives. Plus, when students get in contact themselves, that conversation usually goes into a student's file, making it an important way for that student to express interest in a school as *well* as a good opportunity to get their questions answered.

But most importantly, it's a rite of passage for a young person to learn how to reach out to adults. It's vital, and in many ways a precursor to the types of relationships they'll need to cultivate in university, when they have questions for their professors or need to go to the career center and have somebody help them with a resume. Being able to have an honest, open conversation about their doubts, their fears, the things they don't know or understand, this is an important skill.

"What are you interested in right now?"

"Do you have any questions for me?"

"How did you get interested in that?"

"Can I be helpful in any way?"

"Would it be easier for you if I went with you?"

"Do you think you'd be comfortable talking to that teacher?"

"I'm happy to look over it if that would be helpful."

Young people, as all of us, really fear uncertainty. Some have tendencies toward perfectionism. At the same time, they have been told that "everything matters" for so long, any little (very human) mistake feels like such a BIG thing.

> Realizing that you can't necessarily help in the way that you want but still making sure that your teen has other adults to speak with, whom you trust, is a very healthy way to help them manage the stress of their college applications.

I think it's important for those young people to have multiple adults to whom they can ask questions or express doubts. Adults who know how to speak to them and who understand that doubt and uncertainty are a part of not just this process, but life, who don't shut them down or add to their stress when they express negative emotions, are vital. As a parent, you might not be able to be one of those adults, and that's okay! Realizing that you can't necessarily help in the way that you want but still making sure that your teen has other adults to speak with, whom you trust, is a very healthy way to help them manage the stress of their college applications.

Q: How can my child balance their college applications with their busy senior year?

The ideal way to juggle college applications with senior year responsibilities is making sure you mostly don't have to. The application process is made up of multiple components, and it's very helpful for students to be able to break it up into smaller pieces and make themselves a timeline that they can control. The more a student can cross off their application checklist early on, the more breathing room they'll have in their final year of high school. And in fact, many components of a university application can be completed, or at least begun, before senior year even starts.

Standardized Tests

For example, let's look at the standardized testing component with tests like the SAT and the ACT. We know that many schools are reinstating their testing policies. That means that students who want to get ahead of the process can start taking those tests very early and get them out of the way.

The math portion of the SAT covers Algebra, Geometry, and Algebra 2, material that many students learn by the end of freshman or sophomore years. Therefore, the longer a student waits to take these tests, the further removed they get from the material. This is part of why test prep has become such an industry—young people applying to competitive schools find they need to update their understanding, or refamiliarize themselves, with the material when taking the SAT or ACT.

Students can start this standardized testing process as early as they would like, and take the tests as often as they can. This means that if they take the test early and do poorly, they have plenty of time to improve. On the other hand, if they do very well, they're done. I've had students who finished taking their SAT or ACT exams in 9th grade, purely because the material was freshest in their minds at that time. Having that done so early was a great way for them to set themselves up to succeed in the future—they knew that they'd made progress on the process, and even though the applications themselves wouldn't be starting for these students for two or three years, they were already making progress.

Letters of Recommendation

Another component that we've covered already, but that I'll mention again, is the letters of recommendation. Students can, and should, start establishing relationships with teachers and their school counselor or administrator well before their senior year. After all, recommendation letters are a very important part of a student's application, and the best recommendation letters always come from faculty that have a genuine relationship with a student.

We want teachers to have a strong, authentic, and honest understanding of a student and who they are! To ensure that, students need to connect with those adults. They need to reach out to their teachers, speak up in class, ask thoughtful questions, and generally work to make sure that their teachers and counselors have enough knowledge of them to write insightful recommendation letters that cover things besides the quantifiable information that's already on their transcript.

The other reason these relationships are so important is that counselors can collaborate with students on establishing timelines. If we go back to the question of balancing senior year and college applications, one of the biggest pieces of the puzzle for students is having a *strong* awareness of their timelines and responsibilities. When it comes to things like letters of recommendation, which require involvement from someone else, students need to know what they need and what others need from them, and most importantly *when*.

School counselors and teachers will often have their own specific timelines for when they need to have everything done for all of their student's applications. Counselors need enough lead time to fill out their forms, write their own recommendations, and collect teacher recommendations on behalf of their students. They need to work around different application dates, especially the rolling and early deadlines. For all these things, they're going to need information and prompting from students.

Some school counseling offices have very strict deadlines for students who are planning to apply early. They don't necessarily need to know *where* a student is applying, but they ask for students to let them know of their intention to apply early by a specific date, say August 1st, so that they can organize their time around those students who have the earliest deadlines. If a student doesn't tell them they're planning to apply early, it's possible the school will refuse to let them do so, as there isn't enough time for school officials to fulfil their parts of the application. This is a tragedy which can easily be avoided through communication with one's counselor.

While letters of recommendation don't get written until senior year, students can prepare by establishing those relationships, letting faculty members know that they're going to be asked, and then making an accurate resume of their activities and interests to make the process easier both on themselves and the faculty.

Admissions Essay

Potentially the most intimidating component of the admissions process is the main statement or admissions essay. Note: I do not agree with the term, "personal statement" as it creates a sense that this process is truly a "personal" one. It is not. Nothing about the college admission process is truly personal. Back to the essay, which is very different than what most students regularly do in class, such as the five-paragraph essay. On the other hand, this is creative writing. Storytelling. It's a tale that captures the imagination and transports the reader into the experience. This is a skill that needs to be developed.

If we take a look at how the admissions essay works, admissions systems like the Common Application, or UCAS in the UK, will release a series of prompts for students to work from. These essay prompts are typically released sometime around June of the year of the application process, several months before the application, itself. So, a senior graduating in 2030 will be able to start the actual application in August of 2029, but the main essay prompts will be released in June of 2029, giving that student time over summer to work on their essay.

It's not strictly necessary to even wait until the prompts, as they're only there to give people a jumping-off point. For example, the final prompt option of the Common App is "pick a topic of your choice". Students can think of their own potential topics, or look at prompts from previous years, so they can start brainstorming and experimenting with ideas and building their creative skills and vocabulary. To help with this exercise, I've included a list of first lines that your student can use to brainstorm for their essay at the back of this book (See Appendix C). Once the official prompts do come out, however, I *strongly* recommend that anyone who wasn't working on their essay, begin.

I tell students to set aside big chunks of time during the summer to just sit down at their computers and write, tinker with some ideas, experiment with different prompts, and start getting the essay together. The essay is going to end up taking hours upon hours of work, whether it's in the summer, or in the panicky weekend before the deadline. Being intentional with their time and setting aside those hours during the summer, will help students manage the writing process in a calmer, more creative way.

The Common App is released on August 1st. The actual application asks for basic information about the applicant and can be done in about an afternoon. If a student gets their testing out of the way early, if they have good relationships with their teachers and counselors, and if they work on their essay steadily over June and July, by the time the Common Application comes out, they're most of the way there. They can spend an hour and a half in August filling out the application, plug in their essay, and have completed the principal part of the application for a good 70% of schools in the United States.

At this point, the only thing left would be to follow-up with the school counselor and teachers about recommendations, and then work on any school-specific (supplemental) essays that are required from the individual universities the student has added to their list of schools to which they will apply.

School-specific Essays

School-specific essays are writing pieces that some of the more competitive schools ask for in addition to the main statement. Like the admissions essay, the school-specific essays give students prompts to work from, though the answers required are usually significantly shorter than the main admissions essay.

For my students, I recommend putting the essay prompts from every school into a single document, noting which of the prompts overlap, if any. Usually, multiple schools will ask the same question, or a variation on the same question. Having them all in one place is a good way to make sure that you know exactly how many additional essays are needed.

This final piece of the puzzle is one you can only really work on after the Common App is released in August, which is all the more reason why it's very helpful to get these other parts completed, or at least a fair way along, before then. If a student gets the bulk of this work done before August 1st, they can then really take their time with these school-specific prompts, all the while knowing that for most schools their application is essentially finished. Doesn't that sound like the perfect way to go into senior year?

Q: Are campus visits important?

Campus visits serve two distinct purposes.

The first purpose of a campus visit is demonstrating interest to a university. While you obviously don't have any specific obligation to a school that you visit, choosing to do a campus visit does require a certain amount of commitment from a student and their family. They need to sign up in advance, block off the day, even potentially travel many miles (depending on the university).

Making that effort shows the admissions office that this student is serious about their school, which is something they want to know. Schools want to extend offers to students who are likely to accept them, after all. That being said, a campus visit is far from the only way to demonstrate interest. It isn't even the best way to do so. More on that in a bit.

The second purpose of a campus visit is to give students a more tangible sense of what a college campus is like. There's a lot of things that a student won't really recognize or understand until they've been in the physical space, so a campus visit/tour is a way to start familiarizing themselves.

What you want out of a campus visit is for students to identify qualities they find exciting or comfortable about a school or campus, while gaining insights into things they don't really care about or actively dislike. Maybe they get to a really urban campus and realize they're much more attracted to the idea of green spaces and trees, and they want to be able to sit out on the lawn with their classmates and study outside, etc. That kind of information can be a helpful filter.

Here, I want to emphasize that the idea is not to walk onto a campus and fall in love with it and feel like it's perfect. None are. They're simply places. Schools. Physical structures. The purpose is more to understand how campuses can differ from one another and which of these differences you truly value.

First impressions can be deceiving. Fundamentally, schools are trying to market themselves through their campuses, and they're very good at getting students excited about those spaces. It can be very exciting for a student to walk on campus and see a lazy river. It's a gimmick—if you're paying attention, likely no one is even using that space. But for a student who's looking to fall in love with a campus space, that can be a deciding factor. And that's dangerous.

On the flip side, any little thing could throw off a campus visit, as well. I've had students go to visit schools that should have, based on everything, been excellent. The metrics, my understanding of the student, and of students who had gone there in the past, all of it suggested that this person would have loved that school. But the tour guide was sleepy, or having a bad day, or the weather was bad in a way they weren't prepared for, and suddenly they were miserable and decided this wasn't the place for them. Again, dangerous.

Remember, it's people who make up a university. I'm going to reiterate this: at the end of the day, all that a campus is, is a physical space, a series of buildings. And there are things about that space that might appeal to a student and even figure into their decision, but it's important to make sure those are the right things.

What I think *can* be helpful about a campus visit is getting a sense of the social environment and culture of the school. What happens when you ask people for help? What happens when you say "hi" to people who you're passing? Are people stopping to help? Are people kind and courteous? Are people walking with friends, or by themselves with their eyes on their phones? Do you see students engaging with each other in social spaces?

You can have the most beautiful campus in the whole world, with meditation gardens and redwood groves, but if you don't see anyone using those spaces, that tells you a lot about what kind of environment that school really has. Not the one they're trying to create, but the one that exists.

That's one thing that a campus visit can, in fact, be really good for. But again, these are things you can learn in alternative ways.

What if a campus visit is just not financially feasible for my family?

First off, please let me assure you: your teen will *never* be penalized for not being able to do a campus visit. There are no negative repercussions for students who can't visit a campus, whether for financial reasons, scheduling reasons, or whatever other reason they may have.

Very few families are going to have the resources to take time off, book travel, and go visit universities. Universities recognize the privilege inherent in being able to do a campus visit and many of them are building out accessible alternatives for potential students.

All universities also offer virtual tours. Signing up for these virtual tours is available through the admissions website, which also gives the university a student's contact information and serves as a way for that prospective student to demonstrate their interest, which is the critical piece of this process, from the university side. Like students being able to gain some insight into campus culture and programs, a university gathering a prospective applicant's contact information through registering for an online event, is one way the admission process "commences", from the perspective of the university.

These virtual tours will often offer a Q&A session and group discussion afterwards to give potential applicants the opportunity to ask questions. This is a great time for a student to show their enthusiasm and interest for the school by participating in the discussion. If we're looking at two means of showing interest, taking a physical tour or taking a virtual tour and asking plenty of thoughtful questions that show genuine consideration, the latter will often be considered more valuable. Also, prospective applicants can demonstrate interest by following social media accounts of admissions offices, athletic departments, or faculty from these universities.

Of course, neither the in-person campus visits, nor a virtual tour, are the only good ways to express one's interest to a university. The absolute best way for a student to demonstrate interest is by writing directly to their admissions officer(s) at each respective school.

Most universities have listings of their admissions officers and their email addresses online. If not, there will be a general admissions email address. I encourage my students to find the admissions officer who is the regional representative for their area, and write an email expressing interest and asking thoughtful questions. (As I keep emphasizing, the email should come from the student and not be written by a parent.)

Let's look at a basic template for what this email could look like.

Hi [Insert Admissions Officer's Name],

My name is [Student Name] and I'm a student at [School Name]. I'm in the process of applying to schools and I'm really excited about [University Name]. I did the virtual tour the other day and really liked learning about the campus and the facilities. I was really impressed by [Unique Program on offer/Resource on Campus/Name of Faculty] and it made me determined to learn more.

Could I maybe speak with you or even with a current student who's interested in [Area of Study]? I have some questions and I'd love to talk with someone more about the culture on campus and gain some understanding into personal experiences or insights at [University Name].

Thank you so much for any help you can offer me. I hope you have a great rest of the week and I'd love to hear from you when you have the chance to reply.

Best,
[Student's Full Name]

There are different approaches that can be taken here. What's important is that the student is reaching out, engaging admissions officers in thoughtful conversation, asking them about their experiences, and displaying a wish for further communication. Doing this is not just going above and beyond, it's thoughtful and kind self-advocating. It's a way to show a level of responsibility and maturity, and to demonstrate to the admissions office that the student is engaged.

Admissions officers know that students can't send an email like that to a hundred universities and a hundred different admissions officers, so the assumption is that the student is selecting schools that they're genuinely very interested in, those which they're eager to have follow-up conversations with.

However, I should note that it's important to actually *have* those follow-up conversations. Students need to make sure not to overextend themselves when doing this kind of information-gathering, and parents need to support students in this. There may be a temptation to actually send out 100 of these emails but we must remember that it's not reasonable to do this not because it's 100 emails, rather, it's intended to be the start of a hundred different ongoing conversations.

If a student misses a reply from an admissions officer, that can reflect negatively on them when that officer is looking at their file in the following months. It's important for students to be as organized as possible, have a system in place to track their communication with different schools, and only reach out to those schools they're genuinely interested in.

There's another possible way of expressing interest and learning about a school that I want to touch on, and that's something called an alumni interview. This is where a university will put a student in touch with an alumnus, as a means for that student to be able to ask questions of someone who has, indeed, been in their shoes and can share some wisdom about the university to which this student is applying.

I want to be extremely clear that students do *not* have to do these interviews. They are not weighted in the admissions process. In fact, universities have implemented these, for the most part, as a way to keep alumni feeling involved and engaged with their alma mater. In other words, the benefit to the student is to have the conversation and gain the insight of another's experiences. To the alumni, it's to feel special and a part of this larger community. To the admissions office, it's fairly meaningless.

Because an alumni interview is meant to be an opportunity for the student to hear about the other's own experiences, good and bad, and get honest feedback about the possibilities and opportunities that will be available to them at the particular school, it's really a chance for students to ask the questions on their minds: Did you change your major while you were there? Did any of your core classes surprise you? Are you still friends with your college roommate? Are you still in contact with any of your professors? How did your university or your professors help prepare you for graduate school? Did you use the career center when you were applying for jobs?

> There's a myth that an alumni interview will make or break a student's application, and that simply isn't true.

In this sense, an alumni interview can be beneficial for students. However, the reason I caution students about these interviews is that they don't always go the way they're supposed to. I have heard of more than one instance of an alumni grilling a student about the merits of their application or their goals for the future. When this happens, it's frustrating. Some alumni interviewers don't realize they are doing this to BENEFIT the student and, instead, believe they are somehow acting as a gatekeeper to their prestigious alma mater. Nothing could be further from the truth. It's a lopsided power dynamic and it should not be more terrifying than it already seems to the applicant.

Again, an alumni interview is not about a student's abilities or capacity to succeed. It is not up to alumni to deem a student worthy or not. Parents can put a lot of expectation and weight on these interviews. There's a myth that an alumni interview will make or break a student's application, and that simply isn't true. I would argue that most universities don't even look at the notes that the alumnus sends to the admissions office about their interviewees.

Because alumni interviews can go poorly in these ways, and because this can be very alarming and demoralizing for a student, I don't necessarily recommend them for everyone. Those students who are really interested in doing one should have a clear idea of what the alumni interview is, and what it's not, and ideally go into the process prepared with their questions so they can get what they want- and need- out of the interaction.

What we've discussed so far are alternative ways to express interest when a campus visit isn't feasible. I want to now turn our attention to the other purpose of campus visits: to better understand the university atmosphere and get a sense of which aspects of a campus they find appealing, unappealing, relevant, or not.

Of course, students can, and do, choose to attend schools sight-unseen every year. But I think we can agree that students should be equipped with all the information possible when making such a huge decision about their future. To that end, a virtual tour can once again be a helpful alternative. While the student might not get the full experience of walking around campus, they can at least start to form a mental image of the university and what their life there would look like.

The other thing that a student can do is to visit a local school or multiple local schools that they're not actually interested in. Maybe a student has no intention of going to their local university, but if it's very accessible, and the schools they want to attend are halfway across the country, this can be a great exercise.

That student can go to that local university, get a sense of what the departments look like, talk to other students on campus, talk to the tour guide, and just ask questions: "How did you choose?" "Where are you from?" "Have you changed your major?" "How did you choose your gen ed classes?" Engaging with passionate learners and other people who are undertaking this process is never going to hurt a young person. On the contrary, it might just be surprising how much connection one feels with their local school, with some aspect of a department or program they had not learned about previously, or even how much more certain this helps them become in defining their priorities and hopes for their own campus search process.

Since the idea of such visits is more for a student to build their understanding of what a campus is, not for them to immediately identify their "dream school," it doesn't really matter which schools they visit. Typically, I tell students to visit multiple types of schools when possible. They might go to a large public university in a college town, a large private university in a city, and a small liberal arts school in a rural area. The hope is that they get a better understanding of what these differences look and feel like and extrapolate from there when making the choice between schools they're actually interested in.

So yes, there are elements that students can really only discover by being in a physical campus space. That said, they don't have to be visiting some "dream" school to start to build this understanding. They don't have to get on a plane.

Where I live, there are approximately 12 universities within an hour and a half drive. These schools are all very different. Some are city-based, public, state schools. Some are small, private schools. We have a large research university in a college town near to us. There are just so many.

Of course, I recognize that not everybody will have the same type of access in their area. It's also true that a campus visit might not be doable for your family, whether the university is near or far from you. I am just reiterating that, for those who are concerned about booking a flight and accommodations in order to tour a campus, there are likely some which are much more local that can be a great alternative. In most places, visiting the nearest university will only require a family drive an hour or two.

Trust me, the aesthetic differences between universities really aren't as vast as you might imagine. Dorms are the same pretty much everywhere. Dining halls and athletic facilities really don't change a ton. A track is a track. A field is a field. Yes, there are some differences that will be more important to a student, but they don't necessarily need to see those, in-person, at every school on their list, in order to learn what purpose they serve on a campus and within the community. It's enough for students to visit a local school and begin pulling out features they're interested in, those which they can then take with them as a rubric when doing research, attending virtual tours, and ultimately making their decision.

Q: What is the best use of time for students during their summer vacations?

When parents come to me with this question, especially parents who are driving their children to be high-achieving students, my first concern is to make sure they're clear on what healthy expectations for their child look like. The priority during the summer should be taking advantage of time with oneself, and to nurture relationships with friends and family. Work. Volunteer. Go stay with a grandparent. Take summer classes. Do what you want- or need- during this break.

I think a lot of people believe that being "high-achieving" entails doing a list of specific activities that look good on a college application. They think that there's a code to crack, and as long as the student does the right things, they're sure to get into a good school. And yes, it's true that a student's summer activities can make a great topic for their admissions essay. But there is no secret, no list of cheat codes for conveying in the application process that one is, indeed, a voracious learner. Any summer experience can be turned into a great personal essay if a student is thoughtful and reflective about their activities. That's why, when a student asks me how to appear "high-achieving", I tell them, "I've never met a voracious reader who didn't get into a great school."

Being a growth-minded learner is first and foremost a mindset. I'm not sure "high achieving" is as synonymous with being an open-minded, lifelong learner as some parents want to believe. The former have a fixation on performance and praise, a need to be instructed on what to do, and then they go and do that thing to an almost-painful level of perfection. The latter, on the other hand, have a sincere investment in personal growth and a love for self-directed learning. They take every opportunity to pursue their interests and passions.

There is no secret, no list of cheat codes for conveying in the application process that one is, indeed, a voracious learner.

Individuals who want to grow, learn, and expand their understanding will do so without urging. The real trick is making them take a break. The learners aren't students I worry about when it comes to college admissions. They almost always find the application process, and its outcome, goes in their favor, in large part due to the fact that they treat the experience as another way of growing and learning. It's another difference between a lifelong learner and a high achiever.

I make this distinction because I've met students who don't read at all except for school assignments, who want to get into great schools but aren't very interested in learning, and who want to figure out how they can cut corners and trick the system. This just doesn't work. However, I do believe every student can find this love of learning within themselves. Every student is passionate and interested in something. It's just a matter of reflecting on the subjects and aspects of learning they find exciting and engaging and seeking out ways to pursue those interests.

And so, whenever a student of mine has a vacation coming up. we have conversations about what they've enjoyed reading in the past, what they like to watch, what subjects they're into, and I try to recommend some things they'll love. These can be books, podcasts, documentaries, films. It can be a suggestion to visit a specific exhibit at a nearby museum. These are things they may not have time or energy for during the school year. So, once vacation is in sight, it's a great opportunity for them to complement their learning by exploring topics that they're passionate about and are self-motivated to engage with.

Of course, some students may also wish to expand their summer learning into more tangible activities. They could participate in a math or science Olympiad, they could compete in spelling bees, or submit works for art or photography competitions. They could go to summer camp, or do a summer program (more on pre-college programs ahead), or get an internship in a field of their interest. There are so many different experiences that students can seek out to give them a better understanding of where their strengths are and what excites them.

Again, I'm not telling any student what they "should" do with their summer. There's no one-size-fits-all here. Resources, opportunities, and inclinations will differ from student to student. Some students will work all summer. Some will spend the summer volunteering, coaching a sport, or traveling with their family. All of these are valid ways to spend the summer, and any of them can be the source of a great story for a personal essay.

Should my student be doing community service during the summer?

Community service is valuable for every individual to do. Each of us should be invested in the needs of our community. And when it comes to college admissions, it's true that every applicant is expected to have some amount of community service. Universities expect students to demonstrate it through their activities and through their essays. Does that mean that every student should drop what they're doing and spend their summers volunteering? Absolutely not.

More than anything, schools are looking to see that students are committed to something outside of their grades and test scores. What that commitment looks like, *say it with me*, is <u>different from student to student.</u>

For some students, community service is their passion. Maybe they've racked up 500 hours of community service in high school. Of course, that's very impressive! And most likely their personal essay will focus on that work. But that also describes a very specific person.

If you're a student-athlete, or a musician, or you have a job, or you help with your family, then you're probably not getting 500 hours of community service in high school. You're probably getting closer to 25 hours of community service in your four years. That's okay—you're giving yourself to something else.

What admissions offices are looking for in a personal essay are the things that make a student unique, what their specific commitments are. If a student's commitment happens to be to community service, that's great, the admissions office will love to hear all about it. But if it happens to be to the football team, or the basketball team, or the volleyball team? They'll also want to hear about that. And maybe a student who's really into volleyball just happens to base their community service around a local volleyball group, where they volunteer coach or help out with fundraisers. These are the kinds of things that build a clear narrative about who a student is and can be clarifying for an admissions office.

The last thing I'll say about community service is that students should be doing their community service in their actual communities. Don't fly to the Dominican Republic to help build houses. Stories like that just exude privilege, and they often really rub admissions offices the wrong way. Their (completely appropriate consideration) will be, why did the student have to go all that way? Was there really no way they could have served their own community?

Community service doesn't need to be monumental or world-changing to be important. It's not like universities expect you to be out there saving lives in the wake of an earthquake. That's amazing, but it's not necessary, or even feasible, for everyone to do. What is possible is for everyone to get involved in whatever way they can, for however much time they're able, in their own communities.

Are summer pre-college programs beneficial for a college application?

First off, let's define our terms. Pre-college programs, also known as high school preparation programs, are learning experiences that are hosted by universities, during the summer, for high school students. Students apply for a specific subject, say sociology or economics, and those who are admitted, then take "college-level" classes in that subject, at the university (or online), over the course of 1-3 weeks, sometimes with the promise of earning college credit for those courses.

These programs are pay-to-play. They cost a good deal of money, and the vast majority of students who apply to a program are admitted. They're also not especially useful for a student's application or degree.

Pay-to-play programs are really a way for schools to make money during the summer. They have empty dorms and classrooms, professors on campus, and a dining hall, and they want to take advantage of these spaces and resources. So, they put on these programs, market them as a great form of preparing for university, offer to throw students a college credit for attending, and find someone willing to teach the class.

Some universities don't even run the programs themselves, but rent out the campus to third party companies who put on the programs. Some will have two or three different providers offering summer programs on their campus at the same time.

Students who sign up for these programs don't get to really experience the campus culture. They experience the accommodations and the classes with other high schoolers like themselves. They're not meeting university students; they likely are not even taught by professors from the school.

Now, I'm not saying these programs have absolutely no value. However, any student considering applying to one should know what they can realistically expect. These programs are not university prep, and having one on your application is not particularly impressive to an admissions office. On the contrary, if the rest of the application seems to read like a resume of privilege, adding this to one's list of activities can really hurt them because they are essentially conveying an image of absolute privilege which tends to be the opposite of a thoughtful, self-aware applicant that most universities want.

All this said, of course these programs *can* still be a great way for a student to pursue learning and personal development. If a student is considering engineering but doesn't really have a sense of what that field entails, for example, because they have no exposure to it, a program like this can be a way for them to become acquainted with engineering as a field of study. If, from this summer program, they then realize that they love engineering and want to apply to universities with that major interest, to say their summer pre-college program made a difference would be an understatement. If they find they don't like it at all, that's still very useful information. That being said, an expensive pre-college program certainly isn't the only way for a student to be exposed to subjects in which they are interested.

Ultimately, if the cost of one of these programs is in a family's budget and the student is really interested in the material they've chosen and they're excited to attend, that's a great reason for them to go for it. They might even choose to write their admissions essay about their experience. But if a student wants to sign up for one of these programs because they think it's necessary or important for their application, I'm here to say, save the money and pick up a good book instead.

Q: What should my child know when deciding on early admission?

The first thing to note is that there are multiple types of applications under the "early admission" umbrella (see glossary in page 139).

Before we go into more detail about the benefits and drawbacks to each type of early admission, I want to point out now that early admission is not necessarily a good choice for every student.

Whether a student opts for early decision or early action, the deadline for applications will typically be in November, with responses in December. That means that students should only consider this option if they're completely confident that their application is the absolute strongest it can be in November when they have to submit.

Students who didn't have a strong year in 11th grade or didn't get the score they wanted on the SAT or ACT might want to hold off on applying early. Waiting for the regular decision deadline in January gives them a chance to improve their test scores and to show admissions offices the extra semester, or extra two quarters of grades from their senior year.

If a student does believe that they've put together the strongest application possible and they're interested in applying early, the question becomes how to choose the type of application and which school(s) to apply to.

Of the types of early admission, early decision is the most restrictive. Students may only apply to a single school under early decision. If they're accepted, they are contractually obligated to enroll at that school pending the financial aid offer, of course, for those who seek it. This is even if that student receives acceptances from other schools under early action. Typically, universities send the financial aid offer along with the early decision acceptance, so that a student may more fully understand their costs. This means that a family must also have their financial aid information submitted by the deadline, as well.

This level of restriction can be quite intimidating, but the benefit of early decision is that it gives an applicant a statistically higher chance of being admitted. This is because early decision is as much a tool for the university as it is for the student.

Let me explain, universities are highly concerned with something called "yield", which is the percentage of students who enroll in the school out of those who are admitted. If a school needs 2,000 freshmen, their ideal situation would be to admit exactly 2,000 students and have them all attend. But of course, students are applying to multiple schools and can only attend one, so a university that needs 2,000 freshmen will need to admit 3,000, 4,000, even 10,000 students in order to hit that 2,000 capacity, because they recognize their applicants are typically ap-

Individuals who want to grow, learn, and expand their understanding will do so without urging. The real trick is making them take a break.

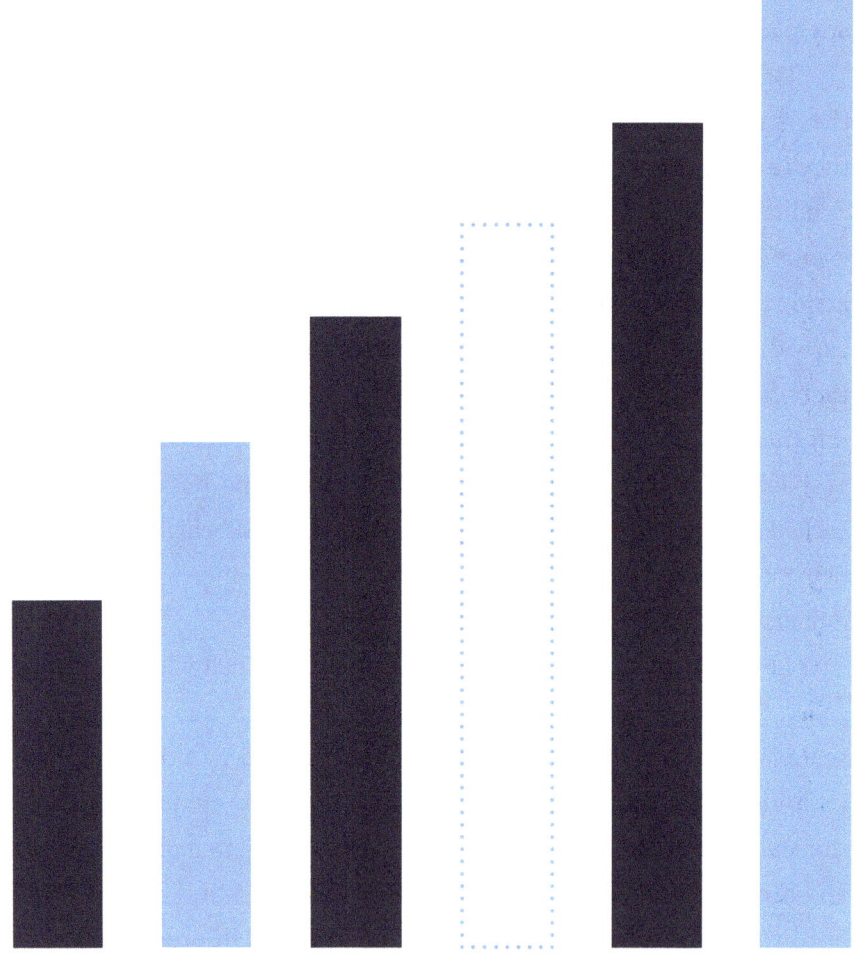

plying to competitor schools, as well.

Low yield reflects poorly on a university, and is a huge part of the U.S. News & World Report rankings. So, if a university has to admit ten people for every one student that enrolls, that leaves them with a 10% yield rate, and this is a real problem for them. This is why early decision has become such an important tool for universities who want to increase their yield. Students who apply for early decision are demonstrating a commitment to that university up-front. Thus, admitting as many students as possible in early decision helps them hit the highest yield percentage possible.

For many competitive schools, where even the most impressive candidates may not get accepted, applying for early decision and showing that commitment can mean the difference between being accepted and not.

Of course, because early decision *is* a commitment, it's also critical for students to choose a right school. One tool that can help them make this decision is their own high school's profile, the one that shows their high school's history with applications and acceptances to universities. The school history is the profile that college counseling offices have access to, and which can illustrate the admissions statistics from your high school. A student can see how many people from their school applied to a university they're considering in the last five years, how many people got in or not, how many applied early versus applying during regular decision.

This is where being realistic about acceptance rates and not becoming fixated on a single "dream school" can be so beneficial. Some universities have acceptance rates of under ten percent, and every single applicant is wonderful. For these universities, it is statistically unlikely for any applicant to get in, but it's even less likely if no one from an applicant's high school has been accepted by- or attended- that university in the past.

What students need to understand about the decision and acceptance process is that it's often one of rejection. Universities reject students for *many* reasons, and if they see that they've never admitted any students from that high school, that can be all they need to validate their decision to reject, thinking, "We just don't know how they'll perform here. We can't admit them."

Given that this is the case, students should use their school profile to their advantage, in order to make the most of their early decision application. Let's say we have a very competitive student, Lily, who is trying to decide between four universities for early decision. She loves all four schools equally, they all have great programs, great communities, they're all in places she'd enjoy living. All four of them are her top choice.

So, Lily meets with her school counselor and takes a look at the school history. She finds out that of her four choices, one of them, School B, has admitted at least one person from her high school, consistently, year over year. Schools A, C, and D, on the other hand, have only occasionally admitted students from her high school. This information leads Lily to decide that School B is the clear choice for her early decision application. Given her knowledge about her high school's history with School B, and the advantage granted by early decision, Lily knows that this will give her the best chance to be accepted to at least one of her top four schools.

Remember, admission is in no way a certainty. Every year I work with students hesitant to apply for early decision because they just don't like the idea of closing off options. When they go for it and get an acceptance, they'll say, "Ah, I should have just applied normally, I would have gotten in."

I'm going to tell you right now, that is typically not true. Even with early decision, the other applicants are so strong, and the percentage of students accepted will be very small. There are many students who will get in through early decision only because they're committing to that school. Had they applied regular decision, they might not have been strong enough candidates to be admitted.

Increasing the chance of admission is the main reason why a student may want to opt for early decision over other forms of early admission. While early action and restrictive early action may still offer *some* statistical advantage for admissions, depending on the school, their main advantage lies in getting information back to students faster.

In a sense, being able to apply early rewards students for having their application done early. Regular decision has a January due date, but it's also a more drawn-out process, with students not hearing back from schools until around March. It can feel grueling. Early action, on the other hand, usually has a November deadline, with students hearing back in mid-December or early January. Hopefully, at that point, a huge weight is lifted off the student's shoulders. They know they have an option for the coming fall semester, and can hopefully enjoy the rest of their senior year without worrying. Even students whose early applications don't go the way they hoped have more information than they did before and can keep it in mind for their next round of applications.

Basically, students who have all their "ducks in a row" can take advantage of early action to try and make their admissions process as streamlined and stress-free as possible.

One warning—different schools have different policies in place around their early admissions processes, such as restrictions on whether early decision applicants can apply for non-binding early action at other schools. Students need to triple-check there are no conflicts if they're planning to apply early to multiple universities.

PART FOUR

Finances

Q: Can a private advisor help our family navigate the financial aspects of college admissions?

Absolutely. The right private advisor should understand the different educational systems and be able to help you create a list of schools that fit your teen's needs while also being in the family budget.

I believe it's very important to establish transparency in this process early on. I know it can be difficult to talk to your children about money. However, if your family isn't clear on the budget, your teen won't have the information they need to make appropriate choices regarding their education. The sooner you have an honest conversation about budget, the sooner your student can channel their time and energy into other aspects of the admissions process. Plus, they might need to know this information when meeting with their school counselor to discuss their plans for college. Information is power!

Budgets create restrictions—you can't eat at a $50 per plate restaurant if you only have $20 for a meal. A private advisor can help your family be realistic about the options within your budget range while also introducing you to options that may be slightly outside your budget, but which have some likelihood of offering some amount of scholarship money.

That being said, there are a lot of misconceptions floating around about the way scholarships are awarded and how common they are. Merit-based scholarships are exceedingly rare. Instead, most of the money that a student can reasonably expect to receive will be based on financial need.

Need-based aid is different than admissions scholarships or merit scholarships. It is not run through the Admissions Office but through the Office of Financial Aid. Although these two offices communicate, they're not the same. One is reviewing the applicant and their admissibility to the institution. The other is gauging what the university can offer to help make sure the admitted students are able to actually enroll.

If you've ever heard of someone saying they received "a full scholarship from Harvard", they are mistaken. None of the eight schools in the Ivy League offer any merit-based scholarships. What they do offer is substantial need-based aid to make sure finances are not a barrier to entry for any student that is admitted to one of their schools.

A private advisor *cannot* help you "game" need-based financial aid. The system in place is fairly foolproof. If anything, it errs on the side of caution, not generosity. (There's a reason we have a student debt dilemma in this country!) If you're paying a private advisor who tells you they can help you get better financial aid, RUN!

As for scholarships, any private advisor who says they can guarantee a student a scholarship is not telling the truth. That's a red flag.

What a private advisor *can* do is offer some insights as to what schools may be most likely to offer some scholarship money under certain circumstances. For example, if you bring me the most impressive applicant imaginable, and instead of having that student apply to the most competitive universities in the country, they apply to a few schools they're "overqualified" for but that have programs they're excited about, there's a great chance they'll be admitted with some scholarship dollars. That's just the way it works.

Let's say you're an outstanding student from California, and you're interested in studying film. When you're applying to private schools, for example, Chapman University and Loyola Marymount University (two of my favorites and amazing for film), these schools will know that you're applying to UC schools and Cal State schools, both systems which are public, and less expensive, for California students.

Based on that knowledge, Chapman and Loyola Marymount might both decide to admit that student, and offer a small merit-based scholarship as an incentive to entice them away from the lower-priced, in-state option(s). These are the kinds of insights that I can offer, but I can't give you a guarantee, and neither can any other private advisor.

If this same family told me their budget is $25,000 per year and not a penny more, we would definitely be shooting for the public universities, knowing that LMU and Chapman would only be options with significant financial aid. Private advisors are concerned with "best fit" universities and not just "best" universities. "Best" is arbitrary, and means something completely different for you than it does for me. In this case, a big part of that difference is financial.

The schools are not going to offer a better financial aid package because you've chosen not to clue your student in to the concept of budgeting for their education. Talk about it with them honestly.

Financial aid and scholarship matter. And that's okay. If you haven't talked about this yet as a family, do it tonight. It's important to be transparent. The schools are not going to offer a better financial aid package because you've chosen not to clue your student in to the concept of budgeting for their education. Talk about it with them *honestly*. And if you need help doing so, a private advisor might be a helpful option.

Q: How can I talk to my child about the budget for schooling?

The process starts with honesty and numbers.

Before you and your student can have any in-depth discussion about the budget, you both need to understand *all* the elements that go into the cost of schooling. To help with this, it's a good idea to first look at the costs of universities that are in-state for you. Get those prices ready, and factor in everything you can, including housing, books, and travel, so you're not just talking about tuition.

Once you have compiled this information, it's time to sit down and go over all of it. Make a document listing the schools you've looked at within different price ranges. Be as detailed as possible so that you can refer back to this document as the process goes on.

With this document in front of you, it's time to have a serious discussion with your teen. Ask them about their goals and hopes for the future. Find out what they're thinking about when they imagine themselves in university so you can use that to guide you as you look at schools within a reasonable price range. Tell your teen what your budget is. Be realistic and be clear that this is a final, non-negotiable number—this is information they're going to need to keep in mind as they make decisions.

Your budget is your budget and there's nothing wrong with that. If that happens to be $5,000, $25,000, $50,000, there is no shame unless we create shame. If the budget is below some of the school options your child is interested in, that doesn't mean they can't apply. There's still need-based financial aid, and merit scholarships aren't out of the question.

If the gap between your budget and the total cost is not too high, there's a good possibility it can be bridged. On the school's part, of course, not your family's. Like I said, a budget is a budget. Stick with it.

Might your teenager be frustrated and confused by the limitations placed on them by the budget? Sure.

But they'll be grateful for fact that you're being honest with them and approaching them with respect. If you treat them like a person who deserves to understand the situation, they'll hopefully reciprocate that maturity by understanding.

Once young people can see the different options in front of them and understand the differing costs, they tend to be open-minded and flexible. Teenagers are reasonable people. We were all teenagers once. Give them grace and kindness. Young people are resilient, and they can make the best of any situation, but in exchange they want—and deserve—to be kept informed of all the factors that are going to impact their future and their education.

Q: What factors should we consider around the cost of schooling?

The question about the cost of schooling is complex, with lot of different parts beyond tuition. Some of these factors are more universal, but it's likely that there will be some financial considerations that are unique to your family's specific situation.

Below I've compiled some of the most common factors that need to be considered when budgeting for university. While this is by no means an exhaustive list, it's a good place to start when you and your child are trying to figure out the options that are realistically within your budget.

State vs in-state schools

One huge factor in the cost of schooling is the difference in tuition costs for in-state versus out-of-state schools. The difference in cost can be monumental, we're talking tens of thousands of dollars.

> Your budget is your budget and there's nothing wrong with that. If that happens to be $5,000, $25,000, $50,000, there is no shame unless we create shame.

The truth is that the University of Michigan, for example, is there to serve the needs of students from Michigan. Its resources and its focus are going to be on students from Michigan. If a student from Georgia applies, they may be admitted, but that doesn't mean that they're going to be offered any way to reduce the out-of-state tuition costs. The way Michigan would see this is, frankly, if you want a less expensive option, go to a Georgia university. Honestly, I absolutely agree.

Many times, students are very excited by the idea of going to school further from home, and they just assume that schools are going to be generous with their financial aid. Don't just assume. There is no guarantee that there's enough to go around, and an out-of-state school is going to prioritize students from within their own state when handing out aid.

We've all heard the story (perhaps, myth) of that one person who received full financial aid to attend some prestigious university. But for every story like that, there are hundreds of students who didn't get the aid they needed, or didn't understand the process well enough and just assumed that every school essentially approached admissions and financial aid identically.

So, if you have budgetary constraints, start by looking at the schools in your state. I guarantee that there are some great options, no matter where you live.

If your student has their heart set on going out-of-state, some schools participate in regional exchange programs (see Appendix B for a list of programs). These are agreements between certain states that allow a student from one state to attend a school in another state at a reduced tuition rate. Keep in mind, not every school in a state participates, and the form of the discount varies from place to place. At some schools the exchange allows students from out-of-state to pay in-state tuition. At others, they just receive a discount, or an automatic "scholarship" of a few thousand dollars to offset a portion of the out-of-state cost.

Do your research when considering one of these exchanges. And again, don't dismiss the benefits of going somewhere closer to home—university is just the next step in the rest of your teen's life. Going into extreme debt to attend a school slightly further away is not worth it.

Financial aid & scholarships

As we've discussed, financial aid and merit-based scholarships are two wildly different beasts. However, both represent a possible way for a university to help reduce the burden that paying for schooling may place on your family.

Aid is disbursed on the basis of need, so you'll either qualify or not. If you need help with the financial aid process, I recommend working closely with an accountant, a school counselor, or a trusted private advisor, or friend to provide all the information that is needed to determine your level of need. There are also many free resources online to help you with your profiles for the College Scholarship Service (CSS) and the Free Application for Federal Student Aid (FAFSA).

The other option is scholarships, which we've briefly discussed. As I said, there are a lot of misconceptions about how scholarships work. First off, the factors that go into awarding a merit-based scholarship is very rarely quantifiable.

The most likely scenario is that the university administration gives the admissions office a certain budget (pot of gold) with a single (but not too simple) directive: bring the most diverse, interesting, creative, thoughtful, dynamic, unique group of freshmen you can get.

To do this, the admissions office takes that budget and awards certain students with incremental scholarships. This might be $4000 per year, $8000 per year, $12000 per year, or $18000 per year, all of which are renewable for the entire four years of a student's degree, pending achievement of a certain GPA.

This is very different than the cultural idea of scholarships that people possess, one which is tied to athletic achievement and totals the entire cost of schooling. Such scholarships do exist, but they're very few and far between, especially for those who are not competing in NCAA Division I sports. Schools which do offer scholarships of that sort, and there are just a few, are typically going to require a lot more work from applicants. Even then, it's possible that such scholarships will still take a student's actual financial need into consideration.

Living expenses, on-campus job opportunities, and more

Most students are going to have expenses extraneous to the cost of tuition. This includes school supplies, and books, as well as travel (both to and from university and around campus), housing, and likely a monthly allowance.

Depending on where the university is, these costs can fluctuate wild-

Young people are resilient, and they can make the best of any situation, but in exchange they want—and deserve—to be kept informed of all the factors that are going to affect their future and their education.

ly. Obviously, the cost of living in a city like New York or San Francisco is going to be much higher than in a college town or suburban location.

At the same time, more urban locations often have greater flexible work options for students, though that doesn't mean there won't be great options for work in more rural locations, as well.

One primary piece of the need-based financial aid process is the opportunity to gain work-study hours on campus. Students who have work study as a part of their financial aid are given priority for on-campus jobs, but usually there are enough jobs available even for those who did not apply (or did not qualify) in the financial aid process. In other words, jobs on campus are typically available for any who want them. It might not always be the most glamorous work, but the work will likely be available.

Often, there are many unique job and research opportunities on a campus. Possibly the most impactful of these in terms of overall cost is the residential advisor/resident assistant/RA position in campus housing. While this job typically comes with a great deal of responsibility, it also offers huge benefits in the form of free (or deeply discounted) housing and meal plans for the student.

I always tell students and their families that if their first year needs to be the most expensive year, that's completely doable. Even though universities typically raise costs each year, once a student is on campus, they have access to all sorts of different ways to make money and lower the overall cost of their education. Another example is scholarships— schools usually have specific scholarships that are only available to current students and not incoming first years. These can be both one-time and renewable scholarships. Typically, a university will have a separate office for these, something like the Office of Scholarship Services, but it could also be served through the more common Office of Financial Aid. Either way, get to campus and ask around!

There are many excellent opportunities that any student can hunt down once they arrive to campus. There are also many wonderful adults on college and university campuses whose job it is to help students navigate these opportunities.

Encourage your student to speak to these employees. They're there to help, and so few students really find them and utilize them to their fullest. Being the one who does can be the difference between swimming in debt and graduating debt free.

Q: Are student loans worth it?

As a general rule, I think loans are an excellent tool for helping afford university.

However, does that mean that a student should take out the full amount of tuition in student loans, for each of the four years of school? Absolutely not.

Student loans should only be considered as a way to bridge a reasonable gap between your overall budget and the cost of schooling. So, if a student has a budget of $10,000 per year and applies for a school that costs $70,000 a year with the idea that loans should cover the rest, that's a dangerous game to play.

But if that same student applies for a school that costs $28,000 per year and receives some merit-based scholarships and grants that bring their total budget up to $25,000, and they want to include a subsidized federal student loan of $5,000 to their package in order to cover the remaining balance and have a little bit of spending money, I think that can be really worthwhile.

The exact number is going to be different for everyone. That said, if it feels like the entire possibility of attending a university is going to be contingent on taking out the bulk of the cost in student loans, I am begging you to look at some lower-cost universities!

University and colleges are just places, made up of people. Remember, every year students transfer out of Stanford, Yale, Harvard, and MIT. These are not perfect communities. For some, they might be worth their price tag. But if it's too much for you, I promise you'll find other great communities of learners.

The most important piece of the university experience is the opportunity to explore different fields and avenues of study. To take advantage of this opportunity, however, a student needs to feel open and focused.

When anyone, but particularly a young adult, is dealing with immense stress about the costs associated with their education, they can get overwhelmed with anxiety. They start to focus more on achieving certain results rather than enjoying the learning process. This can lead to greater emotional turbulence, especially if their results are not what they demand of themselves. Ironically, that turbulence can make it all the more difficult for them to achieve those results.

It's not necessary to avoid loans altogether, but it's important that your teen doesn't plan to go heavily into debt for their education. Encourage them to look at options that are more within your price range and not rely on student loans to make up the larger part of the cost.

Remind them: no matter where they end up going, they're sure to crush it!

A note to parents

Thus far in this book I've been addressing parents directly. But when it comes to the admissions essay, there's only so much help that any parent or guardian, or even friend, can offer. The essay asks students to try to communicate their true, authentic inner selves to the admissions office. It's a big challenge, but one they need to be trusted to tackle themselves.

Which is why I'm asking you, the parent, to pass this next and final part of the book to your teen. Go on. This part's for them.

I'll wait.

PART FIVE

The Teen's Guide to the Admissions Essay

Hi. Let's talk about your admissions essay.

Before you get worried, I'm not here to tell you what your essay needs to be about. I know that students get a lot of (often unsolicited) advice on the admissions essays. The truth is, it's called a personal essay for a reason. You're the only one who can know what the right topic for you is going to be.

Instead, what follows in this chapter is some practical advice for how to get organized, what it means to find a topic that resonates with you, and how to make sure you write the best admissions essay that you're capable of.

Q: How do I begin working on my college essay?

Before you even settle on a topic for your admissions essay, you need to understand what the admissions office is looking for.

Unless you're already inclined to journaling or creative writing, the admissions essay is going to be a very different form of writing than you've encountered before, certainly different than what you're used to doing in the classroom. It's not a five-paragraph essay or a literary analysis—you're being asked to tell an evocative story about yourself, something that gives the reader a thoughtful understanding of you, what you're like, your experiences, the things you think about. You need to seem relatable and interesting and like an asset for your new community. It's going to take practice, and some trial and error, to find your voice and your topic.

Thankfully, there are resources to help! As you're likely aware, every year around June, the Common Application releases a series of admissions essay prompts for the upcoming year. While using these prompts for your essay is not mandatory, they're often a good jumping-off point to start your brainstorming. Plus, prompts from previous years are easily available online to help you familiarize yourself with the types of questions that may be asked—some may even be repeated in the following year. And there's also usually an open-ended prompt so you can choose what to write about if you have your heart set on a specific topic.

Because this isn't necessarily a five-paragraph persuasive essay, you're not going to be able to outline an argument and just go down a list of points.

The advice I give all my students is to set aside some large chunks of time over June and July to develop and write their essay. When you first start out, just sit in front of a computer and do some freewriting. Experiment, try out different first lines and see where those take you.

Look at some of the prompts. There's almost always going to be a prompt that asks you to talk about an activity that's super important to you and why that is. That can be one easy jumping off point for some brainstorming—just try writing about some different activities you do and see if you can pull a compelling, larger idea out of them.

The purpose of this is for you to try-on some potential topics for size and see which you find inspiring. It's also a way for you to expand your creative vocabulary and skill. Your admissions essay should engage the senses—the reader should be able to see, and hear, and touch, and smell, and taste what you do; they should feel like they were really there. Try to push yourself with your descriptive language. If you write a paragraph that you're particularly proud of, try rewriting it but connecting more with the 5 senses.

You might be tempted to squeeze work on the essay into small sprints. But that would be like sitting down to read a book, only to be interrupted every few minutes. You read the same line over and over again, never making any progress. The same thing happens when you try to shoehorn this complex project into little bits of time—you poke away at it without making any progress.

For progress, you need dedicated writing time. I'm talking hours or maybe several days dedicated to this one thing. Take advantage of your free time during the summer, before your days fill up with classes and schoolwork. Remember, this essay is going to take hours of work, regardless. I'm sure you'd rather those hours be done at a relaxed pace, over several weeks in the summer, and not crammed into an entire sleepless weekend right before the deadline.

Sit down and brainstorm, write, rewrite, edit, brainstorm more. It probably sounds like a very intensive creative process, but being intentional with your time will help you make real progress on your essay, and feel in-control during the otherwise stressful, and very uncertain, time of the college admissions period.

The last thing that I'll say is that the essay prompts come out several months earlier than the application opens for a reason. Finishing the essay over the course of two months, before the Common App even opens on August 1st is very doable, especially if you work at it a few hours at a time. After that, the application itself takes barely any time. Imagine what a relief it would be to be practically done with your application before your senior year even starts.

Q: How do I pick a topic for my essay?

Before we can have any discussion of what makes for a good essay topic, I want to take a second to address what your college essay is *not*.

The admissions essay is not an opportunity to brag about your achievements or to count off a laundry list of your best qualities. It is not an avenue for you to talk about how smart and hard-working and impressive you are.

Imagine reading someone's story about winning a Math Olympiad that says, "No one else could solve this problem but I solved it. This reinforced my realization of what a hard worker I am, probably the hardest worker I know. Every time I'm met with a math problem that I can't do, I ultimately figure it out, because I'm resilient and I don't give up."

Chances are that you're making a face right now, and I don't blame you. Obviously, this is a bad way to endear yourself to someone. It's cynical and calculated, it comes across as insincere, and it gives you no way to relate to the writer. But while this example is exaggerated, every year a good 80% of admissions essays approach their topic like this, because students believe it's what you need to do to impress the admissions office.

Don't get me wrong. *Of course,* you want the admissions office to think you're smart *and* hardworking *and* impressive. But that can't be what an essay is *about.* You want your best qualities to come across in the storytelling, so that your reader finishes the essay thinking, "Wow, what an interesting and thoughtful young person."

If I'm an admissions officer, I don't want to read an essay about how great the applicant is. The recommendation letters from the counselor and the teachers are going to tell me all about how great this applicant is already. What I want is to see how well the applicant can communicate their values, their interests, and their struggles to me.

At its heart, the personal essay is how you show the admissions office who you are. It's a way to articulate your point of view, represent your values, demonstrate your thoughtfulness, show vulnerability, and make it easy for your reader to feel like they really know you, at least a little bit. It's also a way to demonstrate your intelligence and love of learning—to show that you have a broader understanding of the world around you, the capacity to build on and synthesize complex ideas, and the knowledge needed to incorporate intellectual thought into your understanding of yourself and your life.

You want to seem relatable and likeable because you want the admissions officer to believe that you will be a good addition to the university community. You also want to make it clear that you're not just a "good student" but a self-motivated learner: someone who is genuinely excited by learning and who will pursue knowledge outside of their classes.

With all that being said, the topic of your essay can truly be anything. It can be about your favorite taqueria, it can be about the first time you crossed a certain busy street, it can be about an argument that you had with a parent, or a sibling, or a friend. Great stories come from every day things that anyone reading can relate to. The potential jumping off points are limitless.

The topic of your essay doesn't matter so much as the framing you choose, and the ideas you bring in. Anything you might want to write about is, therefore, fair game. In the above example of the Math Olympiad, the problem is not the *topic* but the framing of the topic: "I'm great and I won." That same moment can be reframed dozens of different ways.

One student might take that story and write an essay contemplating the extreme competitiveness of our culture and the societal pressures that reduced what should have been a really exciting moment for them into just another line on their transcript.

Another might talk about how they didn't used to like math until they met a teacher that changed their life, and expand that into a reflection on the profound effect a single educator can have on someone's future.

A third might write a slightly tongue-in-cheek account comparing their own win with the depiction of Cady Heron winning the Mathletes competition in their favorite movie, *Mean Girls*, and then use that as a jumping-off point to discuss how movies have become the lens through which young people decide whether or not they're doing their teenage years "the right way".

A good topic might not seem impressive or even particularly interesting in a vacuum. What's important is that you have an interesting perspective on that topic.

I know some students compare themselves with their classmates and worry that they haven't done enough. Maybe they've had to work every summer to help out their family and save for school while their friends have been able to travel, have interesting educational experiences, and focus on creative and intellectual pursuits. Please believe me when I say that whatever you have done is just as important an experience as any other. You have tremendous value. You have stories to tell.

So, what are the specific hallmarks of a good personal essay topic?

First, I highly recommend choosing a story or moment from your life that you think you can write about in a way that transports your reader. This is a creative piece, and you want to be able to use a lot of descriptive language, to tie in a lot of sensory memory, and to relay the many feelings you associate with that moment in a way that your reader will be able to relate to.

> **Please believe me when I say that whatever you have done is just as important an experience as any other. You have tremendous value. You have stories to tell.**

If you talk about awaiting a life-changing phone call, for instance, you could describe your churning stomach, how your palms were sweating as you kept compulsively looking at your phone, the tenseness of your neck and shoulders throughout the day. These details might seem small, but they win a reader over, get them invested, ensure that as they read along, they start to mourn your losses and celebrate your triumphs.

Next, and this might seem obvious, your personal essay needs to be on a topic on which you have actual things to say. Though your essay might begin with a personal story or anecdote, you want to be able to expand that into a more universal point or observation about the world. Admissions offices want to see that you are invested in things beyond yourself, that you think about your community, and that you have an interesting perspective on how your experiences fit into the broader world.

That being said, don't force a narrative that isn't there because you think it's something an admissions office would like. Your story is much more likely to connect if you're genuinely interested in what you're saying. You want to help your reader understand who you are, what you think about, and what you stand for, so choose a topic which actually exemplifies those things. If you don't buy the narrative that you're selling, neither will an admissions officer.

Finally, you want to be able to incorporate your intellectual interests into your story. Maybe you want to talk about a point in history, or an interesting economic theory, a challenging news story that you still think about, or even a book or film that you come back to again and again. You want to show that you're a learner outside of the classroom, and that you're making connections and thinking about the world even when you're not explicitly made to.

To this point, if you're incorporating just one intellectual idea, don't bring in something that is mandatory reading for every high schooler in the United States. *Catcher in the Rye* and *Great Gatsby* are both great books, but if they're the only books you mention, it's going to give the impression that you never read outside of school.

At one point, I worked with a student who was a fly fisherman. His favorite book was *A River Runs Through It*. In his essay, he talked about how fly fishing was something he did with his father, and it was his favorite thing in the world. Despite that, he didn't like talking about it to anyone. He couldn't articulate why he loved it so much, and it seemed slow and boring to other people. Then, he read this book and all of a sudden it gave words and a value to this thing that he'd never been able to properly capture before, and it was the first time he felt really proud of this activity he'd loved for so long.

These aren't necessarily life-altering ideas for an admissions officer, but they're an example of a young person being able to take something outside of themselves and tie it back into their own exploration and understanding. This student could speak very thoughtfully about how this book and this activity altered his beliefs and awareness of the world, and that is something that hopefully makes a reader go, "Wow, what an interesting insight into this person's life."

My last piece of advice on choosing a subject for your essay concerns controversial topics. As I've said throughout this book, your essay can be about anything you want. For some students, the thing that they're most passionate for, and the topic which will give them the most talking points, is politics.

I would never tell you to stay away from politics as an essay topic. However, I do want to caution that while writing creatively about your political ideas or political involvement can be a great use of your personal essay, denigrating or degrading specific individuals and ideas never is.

If you're going to write about politics, make sure you're framing the essay around your own values, beliefs, and experiences. For example, someone could choose to write about canvassing for a candidate and what they learned about the inner workings of our political process. Another student might describe benefitting from social assistance when they were younger and how that helped their family gain enough stability that they were then in a position to volunteer and be the one to help others in-turn.

You don't want the main impression the admissions officer gets from your essay to be one of negativity. After all, they're responsible for making sure that the students they admit will have a *positive* impact on the existing university community. In that sense, a more divisive topic isn't any different from one that's completely uncontroversial. It ultimately comes down to the question of what you want your essay to say about you and whether the topic you choose will help you get that across.

Pick Your Essay Tool

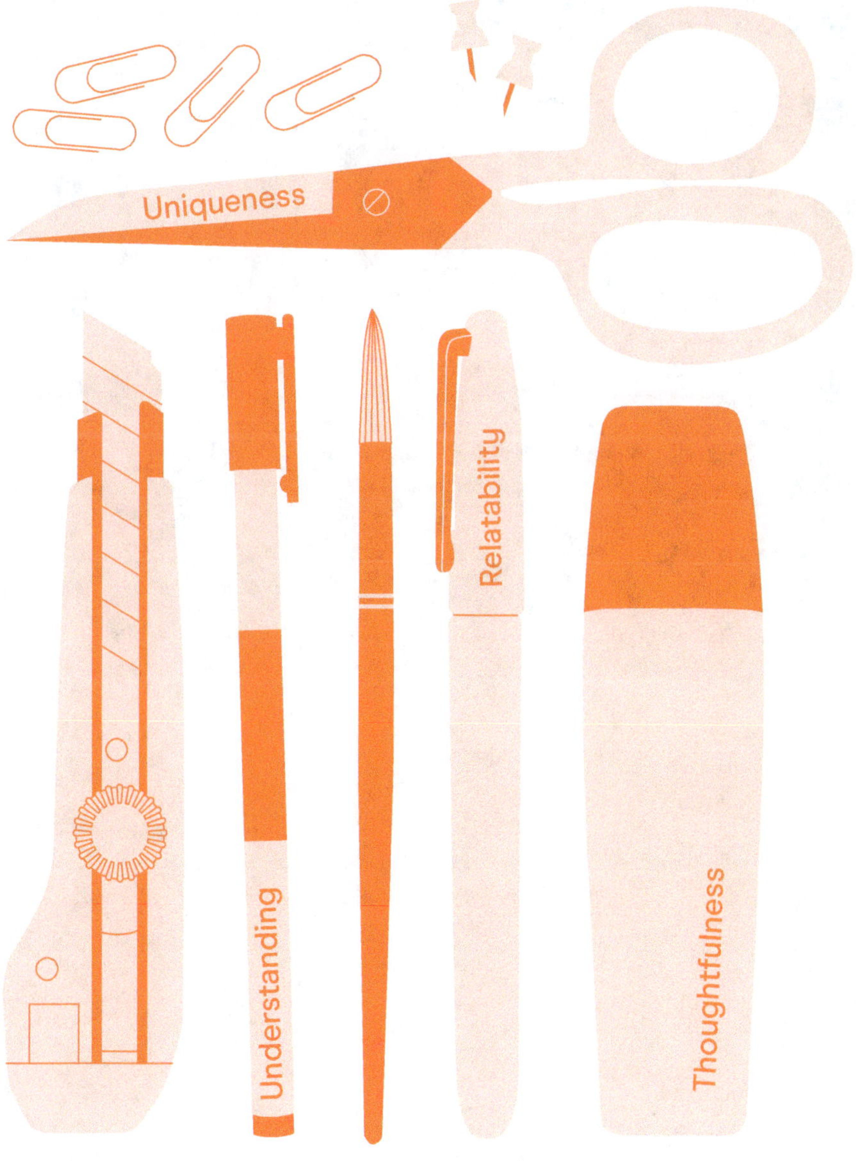
Uniqueness
Understanding
Relatability
Thoughtfulness

Additional Resources

Appendix A – *Regional Private Counselor Organizations* (see page 43)

Appendix B – *Regional College Tuition Discount Exchanges*

Many state schools take part in exchange programs that allow residents of partnered states to attend, without having to pay full out-of-state tuition. If you're interested in attending a school out-of-state, consider asking the universities you're looking into whether there are any tuition exchange programs you may be eligible for.

The four largest of these regional exchanges are:
- Western Region - https://www.wiche.edu/tuition-savings/wue/
- Southeast Region - https://home.sreb.org/acm/participating/institutionstates.aspx
- New England Region - https://nebhe.org/tuitionbreak/find-a-program/
- Midwest Region - https://msep.mhec.org/

More information about Regional Exchanges can be found here: https://www.nasfaa.org/State_Regional_Tuition_Exchanges

Appendix C – *Essay Prompts*

Below, are the 2025-2026 Common App essay prompts. I could be wrong, of course, but I think they're the Common App essay prompts for 2022-2023, 2021-2022, 2020-2021, 2019-2020 ... You get the picture. It's a solid list and starting point.

1. Some students have a background, identity, interest, or talent that is so meaningful they believe their application would be incomplete without it. If this sounds like you, then please share your story.
2. The lessons we take from obstacles we encounter can be

fundamental to later success. Recount a time when you faced a challenge, setback, or failure. How did it affect you, and what did you learn from the experience?

3. Reflect on a time when you questioned or challenged a belief or idea. What prompted your thinking? What was the outcome?

4. Reflect on something that someone has done for you that has made you happy or thankful in a surprising way. How has this gratitude affected or motivated you?

5. Discuss an accomplishment, event, or realization that sparked a period of personal growth and a new understanding of yourself or others.

6. Describe a topic, idea, or concept you find so engaging that it makes you lose all track of time. Why does it captivate you? What or who do you turn to when you want to learn more?

7. Share an essay on any topic of your choice. It can be one you've already written, one that responds to a different prompt, or one of your own design

Now, let's think of some interesting first lines to get the creative juices flowing. Pick one, type it in (or write it down) and go from there. See where it takes you. Imagine. Paint a picture. Hyperbolize. Be literal. Whatever you want, do.

- I had been staring at my computer screen for, what seemed like, hours ...
- For so long, I had found myself in a similar situation, feeling useful/useless but this time was different ...
- There was a moment, just a fleeting moment, where I doubted my choice...
- My nickname used to be (insert here) but when I hit puberty, well, things sort of changed ...
- Being on my own in this situation was definitely new...

- One *could* say I'm an expert at (insert skill here). They could. It wouldn't be the truth, but ...
- It's not always the most exciting time of my day but, on this particular afternoon/morning/evening, "exciting" might even be an understatement ...

Appendix D – *Glossary of application options*

ROLLING ADMISSIONS

When a university reviews applications as applications are received by the admissions office. There are no set deadlines, typically, except for a final deadline which is notably late in the admissions cycle. Don't let that lead to procrastination. The goal of the university with rolling admissions is to fill its class with students prior to that deadline. An applicant wants to submit their application to a rolling admission school as soon as their application is as strong as it can get. No more test scores are needed. No improvement in grades is on the horizon. Every "i" is dotted and "t" is crossed. Some wonderful universities that currently offer rolling admissions include Penn State University, Arizona State University, University of Oregon, Florida International University, and nearly all British and European universities.

EARLY ACTION

When a university sets a firm deadline for applications to be received, earlier than the traditional regular deadlines. Ordinarily, this deadline will be around November 1st but there are a few which have November 15 deadlines or, even, some in December. Regardless, the important thing about Early Action is to remember that it is NOT binding; if the student is admitted, they are not committing to attend. Early Action should be used, when available, only if a student's application is as strong as possible at the time of the deadline. Early Action is useful to applicants, as they get a decision back sooner, typically in mid-December or early January. It is equally valuable to the university admission offices, as they get to spread out the receipt of all applications between these different "rounds". In other words, if a university typically receives 40,000 total applications, during their Early Action round, they can receive up to 10,000 of those, giving them more balance for reviewing all with less time pressure of a single deadline in which every application comes in at the same time. Universities that offer this option are plentiful, including Santa Clara University, Purdue University, Georgia Tech, University of Chicago, and University of Wisconsin.

RESTRICTIVE EARLY ACTION/SINGLE-CHOICE EARLY ACTION

It functions as a combination of Early Action, in that it's not binding for the applicant, and Early Decision, in that it limits them to no other binding applications and offers a slight statistical increase in chances of admission. In other words, a student may choose to apply REA to a school which offers this option, but they cannot then apply Early Decision to another university. Some universities that offer this option (and which I wish would just eliminate it altogether) are University of Notre Dame, Stanford University, Georgetown University, and Yale University.

EARLY DECISION

A binding agreement** that means a student can only apply to one Early Decision at a time. ED should only be utilized when a student's application is absolutely as strong as it can be at the moment of application. An applicant for ED should always be working closely with their school counselor to make sure that the various recommenders are in-place and to gain any other insights the school might have around the ED choices. Ideally, as always, a student doesn't feel like any one school is the "only right school". Thus, they can choose a school that checks many boxes and gives them the greatest potential Early Decision probability of admission. In other words, don't be set on a single school; be open about several schools that fit the various qualities you're seeking. Of course, if a student is absolutely set on a single school, having the application ready by the November deadline, and choosing Early Decision, is very much the best chance for admission. Some schools which utilize Early Decision as an admission option are Williams College, Tufts University, Boston University, University of Miami, and Duke University.

EARLY DECISION 2

The same concept as Early Decision, above, yet it's offered at a later date. This gives applicants the flexibility to either apply to an Early Decision school in the first round and, if not admitted, consider applying to a second school for Early Decision 2, in January. Or, for those students who are still strengthening their application in the August-December time period of their school year, they can still have the statistical advantages offered by choosing Early Decision 2. In other words, if a student really needs to send the grades or scores earned during that period of time, August-December, but also feel comfortable with an Early Decision choice, they have that option with Early Decision 2. Either way, Early Decision 2, like Early Decision, is binding**. Some of my favorite schools which now offer Early Decision 2 are Worcester Polytechnic Institute (WPI), Emory University, Rice University, Vanderbilt University, and Tulane University.

REGULAR DECISION

This is when most universities receive the large majority of their applications. The regular decision deadline varies from school to school, but very few are before January 1 of the year the student plans to enroll. Regular decision has a firm deadline and typically a notification date on which a university will respond to all regular decision applicants. In other words, a regular decision deadline that is January 15 might also release all regular decision acceptance/rejections on a date such as March 15. Unlike rolling admissions, which responds to applicants with an admission decision as each decision is made, Regular Decision schools review all applications in that pool and then release the decisions all at once. Every university offers a Regular Decision option.

**No student is bound to attend a school, even if applied- and admitted- for Early Decision or Early Decision 2, if they require financial aid in order to afford the institution but are not awarded a package which is sufficient for them to be able to attend. In other words, yes, it is binding. But, only if the financial aid needed is what is offered.

Notes

Special Thanks

I have the best job. My former students are people I am so proud to know. They're phenomenal professionals, I'm sure. But they're even better human beings. I am so proud to celebrate them. Always. And this book is just that: a great celebration of the people who have made me the counselor I am. I will continue to devote all of my professional life to mentoring, and being a sounding board for, young people who will become/are becoming adults who wield far greater power and knowledge than I ever will.

Like giving my support to them. So many individuals and families have given theirs to me. In fact, my whole career has been built – this very book has been created – as a testament to that support and mentorship. The list of people who have played a role in this is even longer than the 20 years I have been working in this field. But, as always, there are some special ones who, just in their continued presence in my life, and the lives of my girls, are invaluable:

Duhau
Pelucarte
Salomon
Sanchez
Obando
King
Daneri
 (and Noni)
Watkins
Quail
Enfield
Altuna
Chaplin
Boelter
Sucre
Wiley
Slodarz
Chirinos
Auriemo
Amaro
Pelaez
Campos
Fernandez
Hernandez
Martinez
Madero
Ferezin
Coalla
Bullock
Morales
Escotet
Buffington-Leal

Gutierrez
Mizne
Loureiro
Lake
Civita
Smith
Collett
Gills
Bicalho
Malahias
Cruz
Sada
Rubinsztain
Leal
Olivares
Aguerrevere
Zambrano
Garza
Baldrich
Lanz
Hood
Bilyk
Dachner
Alemann
Rozanski
Bonde
Garcia-Valino
Eseverri
Di Como
Juan Marcos
Giangrande
Miglorancia

Schwam-Marques
Viriato
Maharaj
Pozas
Arguelles
Villareal
Ruiz Maza
Pelayo
Cardenas
Abucham
Duran
Butzer
Lipsitz
Salgado
Tannuri
Ansanelli
Carbone
Sapoznik
Vella
Capriles
Cohn
Rincon

For my very first student, *Danny Guevara*, you are loved and missed.

To amazing coaches: *Ray, Darl, Mosher, Gord, Willy, Wagner, Dianna.*

For *Armchair Expert: Experts on Expert*, the podcast I recommend to every young person.

Jofi, you really lift me up and were the first to say that a book I write would have value.

Thanks to *Jane Tabachnick* for your support with the storytelling, and positive ... everything.

Thanks to *Lori*, for the artistry and professionalism in seeing this book as something valuable and then making it more valuable with your design mind (and all the Sucre-Pantin web of awesome)!

Thanks to *Deb Lake* for your invaluable feedback and family friendship.

To my Brazilian family, *Cris, Andre, and Johnny.*

To my close counseling friends, especially *Barry, Augusto, CW, Iris, Marcela MM, Christie C., Dan M., and Becky K.*

Nathan Maasz and Sarah Wintermeyer with TrioPrep, the most competent and compassionate tutors in the business.

To all the university admission officers and high school counselors who bust their butts every day to make this process better for young people by being kind and compassionate (and who push for transparency).

Alldredge, Pearl, Abe-Youssefi, Mink, Ellen, Purcell, Lianne, Krueger-Devine, Mick, Nesting, Sanbongi, Sharron, Fedele-McLeod, Tessier, Perry-Kenyon, Barnhart, Wisniewski, Facey, Wintzer, Straw-Harwood, Radin, Clevenger, Lulia, Shobhana, and Sanjana. I love you all.

Mom, Jack, Casey, Maureen, Kenneth, Jeff, Margaret, Cyn, Dad, Camille, Auntie, Deb, Julie, Bill, Mike, Madi, Sebastian, Em, Hayden, Gaia, Dirk, Mel, James, Madelyn, Emma, Erik, Sam, Erin, and Thomas. I love you.

To my wife, *Lucy,* who makes my life wonderful, and this career possible, in every way. I'm still convinced it only ever started successfully because people liked you so much!

To *Lily and Luna,* our daughters, who make me laugh forever, and grateful even longer. You are the muchy much that my soul always needs. I am always so proud to be your dad.

About the Author

As Norvall has been a school counselor, and an advisor (independent of a school), as well as a former NCAA Division I university coach and recruiter, his book is informed by more than 20 years of work with young people (and their families). Education choices, transitions, and opportunities do not have to be excruciating. In fact, the positive impact that higher education can have on those who approach it with the right support and mindset is limitless.

Photo by Laura Sucre

www.ingramcontent.com/pod-product-compliance
Lightning Source LLC
Chambersburg PA
CBHW061804120626
46550CB00005B/2129